GEOLOGY AND LANDSCAPE
IN BRITAIN AND WESTERN EUROPE

GEOLOGY AND LANDSCAPE
IN BRITAIN AND
WESTERN EUROPE

DAVID JOHN, RICHARD MOODY, and DAVID ROLLS

OXFORD NEW YORK TORONTO

OXFORD UNIVERSITY PRESS · 1983

Oxford University Press, Walton Street, Oxford OX2 6DP

London Glasgow New York Toronto
Delhi Bombay Calcutta Madras Karachi
Kuala Lumpur Singapore Hong Kong Tokyo
Nairobi Dar es Salaam Cape Town
Melbourne Auckland

and associates in
Beirut Berlin Ibadan Mexico City Nicosia

Oxford is a trade mark of Oxford University Press

British Library Cataloguing in Publication Data

John, David
  Geology and landscape in Britain and Western
  Europe.
  1. Landforms — Europe, Western 2. Geology
  — Europe, Western
  I. Title II. Moody, Richard III. Rolls, David
  551.4'094   GB437.E/

  ISBN 0-19-217686-2

Library of Congress Cataloging in Publication Data

John, David.
  Geology and landscape in Britain and Western Europe.
  1. Geology — Great Britain. 2. Geomorphology — Great
  Britain. 3. Geology — Europe. 4. Geomorphology —
  Europe. I. Moody, Richard, II. Rolls, David.
  III. Title.
  QE261.J64 1983   554   83-13179

  ISBN 0-19-217686-2

Set by Oxford Verbatim Limited
Printed in Great Britain by
The Thetford Press Limited
Thetford, Norfolk

Contents

Acknowledgements

All diagrams have been drawn by Linda Parry. The following are based, in whole or in part, on the sources indicated:

Fig. 3: Sherlock, R. L. *London and Thames valley* (British Regional Geology) 3rd edn. HMSO, London; Fig. 6(a) (b): Debelmas, J. *Géologie de la France*. Doin (1974); Fig. 7: de Lapparent, A. F. *Région de Paris*. Hermann, Paris (1964); Fig. 8: Tricart, J. *La partie orientale du Bassin de Paris* Vol. 2, SEDES, Paris; Fig. 9: Rat, P. *Bourgogne-Morvan*. Masson et Cie, Paris (1972); Fig. 10: Martonne, E. de *The geographical regions of France* Trans. H. C. Brentnall, 2nd edn. Heinemann, London; Fig. 11: Debelmas, J. *Géologie de la France*. Doin (1974); Fig. 12: Blanchard, R. *Les Alpes occidentales*. Arthaud, Grenoble (1956); Fig. 13: Debelmas, J. *Géologie de la France*. Doin (1974); Fig. 16: Gabert, P. *Les plaines occidentales du Po et leur piedmont*. Ministère de l'éducation national et du centre national de la recherche scientifique, Paris; Fig. 17; Roberts, B. *The geology of Snowdonia and Llyn: An outline and field guide*. Adam Hilger, London (1979); Fig. 18: Williams, D. and Ramsay, J. G. *Geologists' Association Guide* No. 28 (1968); Fig. 24: Drawn from an air photograph. Aerofilms, Ltd., Ref. A77901; Fig. 25: Embleton, C. *Snowdonia* (British Landscapes through Maps). Geographical Association, London; Fig. 38: Orme, A. R. The raised beaches and strandlines of South Devon. *Field Studies* **1** (2); Fig. 39: Peterlongo, J. M. *Massif Central*. Masson et Cie, Paris (1972); Fig. 40: Peterlongo, J. M. *Massif Central*. Masson et Cie, Paris (1972); Fig. 60: Hansen, S. The Quaternary of Denmark. In *The Geologic Systems – The Quaternary. 1.* (ed. K. Rankama). Wiley, London (1965).

All photographs are from the RIDA Photo Library. The following photographers are acknowledged.

Bayliss, D.: Fig. 34; Maltman, A.: Figs. 19, 20; Moody, R. T. J.: Figs. 14, 15, 27, 41, 43, 46, 48, 50, Plates 1, 2, 5, 6, 8, 11, 12, 13, 14, 15; Kay Strand Peterson: Fig. 61; Rolls, D.: Figs. 21, 22, 23, 29, 30, 31, 32, 37, Plates 3, 4, 7, 9, 10; Towse, R. Fig. 35.

We thank the many colleagues and friends who have supplied information and data and so helped in the completion of this text.

Plates

(Plates fall between pages 84 and 85 of the text.)

1 Looking south from the escarpment of the North Downs at Newlands Corner near Guildford.

2 Jurassic sediments of the Boulonnais with cross-stratification and ferruginous lenses.

3 Solution pipes in Chalk, northern France.

4 View overlooking the Cirque du Fer à Cheval.

5 The French–Italian Alps looking north-east from the base of Mont Blanc.

6 Polished and grooved rock surface in the valley of the Dora Baltea.

7 Morainic landscape around Llyn Idwal.

8 Fossil-ripple marks in Lower Palaeozoic rocks of the Capel Curig region of Snowdonia.

9 Heathland dominated by common heather or ling, the New Forest.

10 A granitic tor of south-west England.

11 Volcanic landscapes of the northern Chaîne des Puys, seen from the slopes of the Puy-de-Dôme.

12 View from the west-facing slope of the Puy-de-Dôme showing typical landscape elements of the Auvergne.

13 Unconformable junction between basement rocks and boulder bed. Playa de Pals, Costa Brava.

14 A view up the valley of the River Llobregat.

15 A view towards the so-called Camel Rock of the Montserrat mountains.

Introduction

You are looking at a landscape: what do you see? The immediate impression is probably of a kaleidoscope of colours and patterns. To understand them requires an appreciation of the complex interplay between the mantle of vegetation and Man's activities. Now use your imagination to remove these features. Fresh themes then emerge for investigation. First, the shape of the land itself is more clearly seen, and in the more spectacular regions questions about its origin immediately arise. It is often possible to go a stage further and to examine the geological materials that lie below the land surface, and on which the superstructure of scenery is built. These three approaches to landscape investigation – vegetation, land-forms, and geology – require an appreciation of the great differences in time spans that may be involved. A tree, a hundred years old, may be set in a landscape whose basic shape was carved a million years ago on rocks which may be hundreds of millions of years old.

The rocks exposed at the Earth's surface have preserved within them an imprint of the processes that were active during their formation. To decipher them we need to observe the geometry of the outcrop and the rocks themselves in hand-specimen. Red sandstones with dune-bedding, for example, indicate terrestrial conditions; limestones with corals and associated fossils represent the former presence of warm, carbonate-rich seas in areas where town and villages now stand. In many outcrops we can see fractures (faults) and folds. These structures provide information on periods of crustal disturbance and mountain-building. Volcanic rocks and granites are further proof of the Earth's internal activity. In the cores of mountainous areas and in areas of great antiquity highly altered metamorphic rocks reveal how changes in temperature and pressure affect the chemistry and texture of sediments and igneous materials. It is therefore possible to obtain from rocks information on the climates, geography, and the distribution of life in the remote past. They also provide information on the composition of the Earth's inner layers and the mechanisms that affect the continental crust.

The scenery we see today is the latest stage in a long history of development, dominated by the varying action of agents of erosion on the underlying rocks and structures. Investigations of the origin of scenery are based upon these three elements of geology, surface processes, and time. A useful starting-point is a geological map, which may suggest immediate explanations for scenic features. A conical hill may, for example, be caused by recent volcanic activity, while a long steep slope, or escarpment, may be a consequence of dislocation in the Earth's crust. A second major clue is provided by a study of the ways in which the work of erosion is carried out. Many landscapes are stamped with the distinctive results of the major agents of erosion. The valleys of the Alps, carved by glaciers, contrast with those of south-west England where rain and rivers have been the chief sculpting agents. The shapes of land surfaces also vary with the length of time that erosional processes have been at work. A wide, gently sloping valley suggests a long period of river-based erosion; a narrow gorge indicates a short history of rapid incision. In western Europe there is abundant evidence that the nature of the erosional processes has changed several times in the same area during the past two million years. Valleys lacking streams in the chalklands of north-eastern France are evidence that more surface water was available in the past, and the same area is widely covered by rock debris resulting from arctic conditions.

Vegetation and farmland are ever-changing elements in the physical landscapes of western Europe. Both reflect a long history of evolving land usage, superimposed upon, and conditioned by, a complex interrelation of geology, relief, and climate. Thus, in any one place, the present scene probably differs significantly from those of previous centuries, although the precise blend of continuity and change will vary with local circumstances. Unravelling the relative importance of these natural and human influences can add interest and depth to landscape appreciation. The analysis may be attempted at different levels of generalization. As a starting-point, it is first necessary to realize that until 5000 to 6000 years ago, before the spread of the earliest farmers into western Europe, nearly all the land was under forest. The fragments of forest that remain are usually confined to places that proved unsuited for agriculture, and with few exceptions they are much altered in their ecological character and balance of species. Farms replaced the forest on the better soils, but wherever soil or terrain were not suited to farming in the strictest sense, common grazings in the form of moors, heaths, and downs came into existence. Increasingly, however, the common grazings are being improved for agriculture and afforestation, or otherwise used as areas of recreation and amenity.

We can now apply these principles to the investigation of European scenery, basing our method on the ways in which man has traditionally explored new regions. The first investigations have often entailed a journey across a new area, and we are repeating this approach, which will bring out the character and diversity of the scenery of western Europe. Detailed regional investigations have usually followed such exploratory journeys. We have thus selected six regions that, as well as being scenically attractive and popular in their own right, make up a representative selection of European landscapes.

Bibliographical note

Our descriptions of most of the following landscape features are based either on our own observations or on articles in the specialist journals. The following books provide a more general introduction to the geology and scenery of north-west Europe.

Books that provide introductions to land-forms, geology, soil, and vegetation

Bloom, A. L. (1978). *Geomorphology*. Prentice Hall, Englewood Cliffs, New Jersey.
Bridges, E. M. (1970). *World soils*. Cambridge University Press.
Dury, G. H. (1970). *The face of the Earth*. Penguin, Harmondsworth.
Eyre, S. R. (1968). *Vegetation and soils – a world picture*. Edward Arnold, London.
Hamblin, W. K. (1978). *The Earth's dynamic systems*. Burgess, Minneapolis.
McKerrow, W. S. (1978). *The ecology of fossils*. Duckworth, London.
Read, H. H. and Watson, J. (1968). *Introduction to geology*. Macmillan, London.
Reading, H. G. (1981). *Sedimentary environments and facies*. Blackwell, Oxford.
Sparks, B. W. (1971). *Rocks and relief*. Longman, London.

Books covering the journey and the regional accounts

Ager, D. V. (1981). *The geology of Europe*. McGraw Hill, New York.
Houston, J. M. R. (1964). *The western Mediterranean world*. Longman, London.
Monkhouse, F. J. (1974). *A regional geography of western Europe*. Longman, London.
Squyres, C. H. (1976). *Geology of Italy*. Earth Sciences Society of the Libyan Arab Republic.
Shorter, A. H., Ravenhill, W. L. D., and Gregory, K. J. (1969). *South west England*. Nelson, London.
Steers, J. A. (ed.) (1964). *Field studies in the British Isles*. Nelson, London.
Tansley, A. G. (1968). *Britain's green mantle*. (2nd edn). George Allen and Unwin, London.
Wooldridge, S. W. and Goldring, F. (1953). *The Weald*. Collins (New Naturalist), London.

The following more specialist regional guides are helpful in the study of specific areas.

Guides Géologiques Régionaux de la France. Masson et Cie.

Alpes. J. Debelmas.
Bassin de Paris. Ch. Pomerol.
Bourgogne-Morvan. P. Rat.
Jura. P. Chauve.
Massif Central. J. M. Peterlongo.
Région du Nord. C. Delatre.

Geologists' Association Guides.

No. 10   *The north coast of Cornwall from Bude to Tintagel.*
No. 14   *Southampton district.*

Introduction

Memoirs of the Geological Survey of the United Kingdom.

Geological maps of the various regions dealt with in this book can be purchased at good bookshops in the countries of origin or in the United Kingdom from Browns, 160 North Gower Street NW1 2ND, and Stamfords, 12 Long Acre, WC2.

Of the many plant identification texts available for the regions dealt with in the book, perhaps the two with the most general value are:

O. Polunin (1972). *Flowers of Europe*. Oxford University Press.
O. Polunin and Everard, B. (1976). *Trees and bushes of Europe*. Oxford University Press.

1 A journey through Europe

Introduction

Drive from Britain to the Mediterranean and you will pass through a landscape mosaic that provides a representative sample of the scenery of western Europe. The particular journey we have selected, between London and Genoa, is designed to introduce a wide variety of landscapes and to show how their origins may be investigated. The development of scenery is partly due to the ways in which Man has, over the centuries, moulded the environment to his own needs, but at a more fundamental level it is a response to basic geological controls. Our jouney has therefore been divided into a number of geological provinces which give a unity to the sometimes bewildering array of scenic units.

The London Basin and the Weald

The City of London may not seem a natural starting-point for examining the rocks and scenery of the London Basin (Fig. 2) but in fact it offers several important clues. The first impression may be of tall office blocks, hinting at a strong, consolidated bedrock to carry their weight as is the case with New York, for example. Closer inspection, however, suggests that these buildings are of very recent construction, and that most development within London has been to quite modest heights. The recent and rather sudden upward expansion suggests than new engineering techniques have been introduced to overcome inadequate foundations, which in turn imply relatively weak rocks. The history of building in the London area indicates that there may be some variety within this rather weak bedrock. The earlier settlements were built on the higher, well-drained areas, on sands and gravels, while the last areas to be exploited were low-lying and poorly drained, on clay.

The shape of the land surface within London indicates that the forces of erosion have had a surprisingly complicated history within the basin. From a high vantage point, such as the Post Office Tower or the National Westminster Tower, the general impression is of an almost monotonous landscape, with occasional low, flat-topped hills, which hardly seems to repay investigation. More detailed study, however, hints at a remarkably complex history. From our vantage point we can see the high ground of Hampstead Heath standing at 123 metres. This is developed on sands and gravels of the Eocene Bagshot formation, which crop out extensively in the central area of the basin and form wide heathlands in Surrey and Hampshire. If you walk on Hampstead

1

A journey through Europe

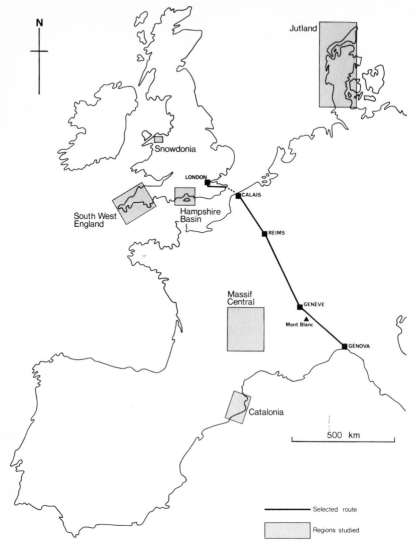

Fig. 1. The route from London to Genoa and the six regions described in Chapters 2–7.

Heath you can see the constituents of a thin layer of gravelly debris mantling the Bagshot Beds at this locality. This debris is ancient river gravel, containing dark, rounded flints derived from the underlying Eocene rocks, together with chert, a rock rather like flint. The chert, however, can have originated only in the Lower Greensand of the Weald, and its presence on Hampstead Heath suggests that a stream, possibly an ancestor of the Mole (a southern tributary of the Thames), flowed to join an early Thames well to the north of its present line.

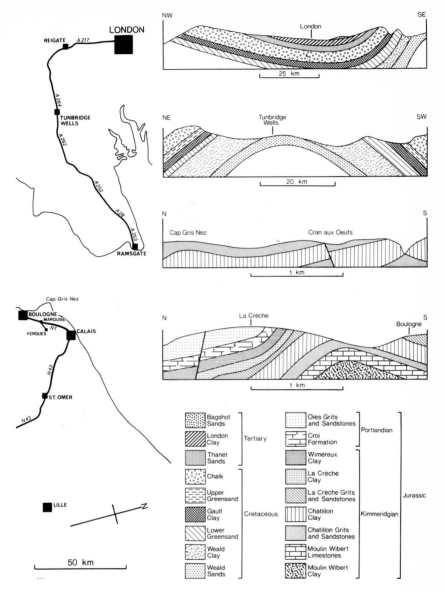

Fig. 2. A section of the chosen route from London to Genoa with geological sections to illustrate the form of the London Basin, the Weald, and coastal sections between Calais and Boulogne.

A journey through Europe

One can study later episodes in the history of the landscape by walking from Hyde Park towards South Kensington along Exhibition Road (Fig. 3). Here we pass across an intricate piece of scenery left by an ancient, Ice-Age Thames. Three land-form units can be identified: the generally flat surface of Hyde Park, a much steeper section south of the Royal Geographical Society's building in Kensington Gore, and a further flat unit south of the Geological Museum.

Most rivers in the lower part of their courses have a flat spread of sediment, entering on either side of their channels. This is called a flood-plain. If for some reason a river incises its channel, a former flood-plain may be left behind as a terrace standing some way up the valley side. This is exactly the case with the ancient Thames. Between Hyde Park and South Kensington there are two ancient flood-plains, separated by a change in the angle of slope, or break of slope. The Thames has left behind a widely developed staircase of former flood-plains within the London Basin, especially north-east of Maidenhead. A study of their shape, and of the river debris they contain, has produced a complicated picture of a stream swinging across its valley in response to varied Ice Age episodes. Even in central London it is possible to understand the main features of the landscape, but it is easier to appreciate the character of the rocks if you travel towards the Channel. The older rocks, the Lower Tertiaries, crop out in the Charlton district near Greenwich where, until recently, it was still possible to study their relationship with the underlying Chalk.

The upper surface of the Chalk in this area was eroded in early Tertiary times, and the presence of a distinct pebble bed (ancient beach) was seen to represent an advance, or transgression, of the sea. The junction between the Chalk and Tertiary rocks near Charlton clearly represents a break in deposition between rocks of different ages: an unconformity. The sequence of sands and clays above the pebble bed suggests that the subsequent sedimentation was rhythmic, with alternating advances and withdrawals of the sea. Within this section various fossil-bearing horizons provide important clues to the ancient environments. The presence of certain clams or bivalves, and a leaf bed, are good indicators of the former existence of offshore lagoons in this part of London. At Charlton the upper sands contain marine

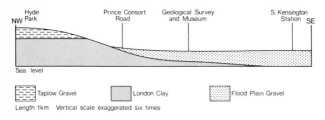

Fig. 3. Section through part of Central London showing two spreads of river gravels ('Taplow' and 'Flood Plain') left by the early Thames.

4

fossils, but their abundance is limited by comparison with those found in sediments of similar age at Abbey Wood near Erith. Bivalves are again the most common fossils, although sharks' teeth and turtle bones are frequently found.

Further south-east, on the Isle of Sheppey, there are exposures of a stiff, generally glutinous sediment that weathers brown on prolonged exposure. This is the London Clay, which is essentially the middle member of the Tertiary sequence present in the London Basin. As it is such a soft rock, exposure is rather uncommon, but we can in many places infer its existence from indirect evidence. For example, it gives rise to low, flat, poorly-drained terrain dominated by pasture land and oak woodland, It crops out over a wider area than the other Tertiary beds, and is found underlying extensive areas of Essex, together with the south side of the Thames towards Croydon, and extensive areas in the region of Windsor.

Near Epsom, a south London suburb, the general slope of the land surface gently rises in a southerly direction. Our route now passes over rolling, chalk countryside. There are many valleys with quite steep sides that show no sign of any activity by present-day streams. These are the well-known dry valleys of the Chalk. They may be quite old, and were perhaps cut in early Tertiary times, then filled with sediment, and finally exhumed during the past few million years. There are similar features on the margins of the Weald and we shall give an alternative view of their formation when we come to discuss them.

The crest of the North Downs defines the southern margin of the London Basin, and looking back towards London confirms that we have been travelling up the dip-slope of the Chalk. If we now retrace our journey in imagination we can visualize a great sheet of chalk descending northwards. A visit to the Chilterns would demonstrate that the same rock rises once again to the surface. The Tertiary sands and clays therefore occupy the inner areas of a basin or saucer-shaped structure: a syncline.

At many places along the crest of the North Downs you will find, if you inspect the ground closely, that you are separated from the Chalk itself by either a cover of sandy sediments or, more usually, a veneer of flinty clay that often appears to rest on a planed-off land surface. The pebbles from these sediments are well rounded and their surfaces show a network of crescentic scars. However, unlike Eocene pebbles, they are occasionally cleanly broken, and many are much lighter than the almost blackened pebbles in, say, the Bagshots.

These flint pebbles are believed by some geologists to have been rounded and scarred by wave action on a late Pliocene shoreline some two million years ago. On this hypothesis the whole landscape of the basin has been developed since that time, as the sea steadily retreated from its high level at about 200 metres.

The gentle climb up the northern slope of the North Downs marks the transition from the London Basin to the southern structural unit called the Weald. From the crest of the Downs the ground falls steeply away to the south, (Plate 1) and this striking contrast in gradient reinforces our view that the Chalk dips gently northwards. This asymmetrical Chalk upland is called a cuesta, and we shall meet many examples between London and the Mediterranean.

Looking south from the crest of the Downs, we can in imagination project the Chalk beds in the form of a great mid-air arc, which finally descends away to the south at the line of the South Downs. We have then defined a dome-like structure or anticline (note the contrast with the London Basin, Fig. 2), which may originally have been as much as 1000 metres above sea-level at its summit. If you consult a small-scale map of the Weald you will see that the highest central point is Crowborough Beacon, at 238 metres, while towards the northern margin Leith Hill reaches 290 metres. Through erosion, the original dome has been largely gutted, exposing the internal structure of the Weald and revealing a number of different rock-types, each of which gives rise to its own distinctive local landscape.

Much information may be gathered by a careful examination of the countryside that is visible looking south from our vantage point. The steep Chalk slope, or scarp, in the foreground is pock-marked by quarries that reveal the bedrock, and is often indented by dry valleys. Many of these valleys are the result of conditions towards the end of the Ice Age, when seasonal thawing gave rise to torrents of water that bit into the still-frozen underlying rock. Great volumes of chalk debris were shifted during this period, and you can see samples of this material, called coombe rock, resting on the solid rock at the top of many quarries. As the climate became warmer surface flow ceased, and the valleys dried out. At certain places along the scarp foot, such as between Oxted and Dorking, there is a raised platform, or terrace. This feature, which often supports prime agricultural land, is developed across the resistant Malmstone of Upper Greensand age.

In the middle distance and stretching away to the east and west a wide valley can be seen. This coincides with the outcrop, or strike, of the soft Gault Clay, and so is termed a strike vale. This rock is generally poorly exposed, but at Squerrye's Pit near Westerham you can see grey-green clays in which many fossils of marine creatures have been found. The Gault rests on the upper layers of an older formation, the Lower Greensand, which can be examined in more detail at Sundridge, a few kilometres from Westerham. Here you can see sandy limestones (Kentish Rag) and loam-rich sands (Hassock). Many fossils have been found in these sediments. The presence of rather sharp folding shows that the Weald is a more complex structure than the London Basin.

From a viewpoint on the Chalk crest the characteristics of the wooded, hilly country developed on the Lower Greensand rocks can be examined. We are here looking at a further, classic example of a cuesta. The tough

6

formation that caps this land-form near Westerham is the Kentish Rag, but further west it is replaced by the Hythe Beds. Beyond Dorking the Hythe Beds contain chert bands whose resistant nature gives rise to the most spectacular cuesta scenery of the Weald. The north, or back slope, is cut by a number of dip valleys; the steep southern slope has been subject to land-sliding over the underlying Weald Clays.

If you wish to see the central area of the Weald, and to examine more examples of the relationship between rock type and land-form, you should continue south from Sevenoaks towards Tonbridge along the A 21. Just below River Hill, on the scarp of the Lower Greesand cuesta, you will pass over a broad, rather monotonous plain formed by the Weald Clay across which streams such as the Medway wind sluggishly. At Tonbridge the underlying geological material changes to the resistant Hastings Sandstones which, together with some clay horizons, make up the core of the Wealden dome. The road now climbs steadily towards the High Weald, often crossing extensive areas of heathland, which reach their finest development in Ashdown Forest. The scenery is dominated by flat-topped sandstone ridges separated by steep-sided valleys (gylls) with level, sandy floors.

If you continue this diversion southwards you would pass, in reverse order, the sequence of rocks you have already encountered. Notice, however, that the Lower Greensand cuesta has almost vanished, due to the absence of a resistant horizon, and that the steep slope of the Chalk cuesta of the South Downs faces north. This provides convincing evidence of the dome-like structure of the Weald.

Although this diversion offers a fine demonstration of the land-forms developed in an eroded dome, the route followed by the A 25 from Sevenoaks towards the Channel ports of Dover and Ramsgate provides many detailed examples of the scenery associated with strike vales and cuestas.

The London Basin and the Weald are geologically and morphologically opposites but they share certain basic types of vegetation and farmland. Heathland, for example, often with dark blocks of conifers, is very common in both regions. The briefest examination will reveal that it is nearly always associated with tracts of sand or sandy gravels. Regardless of age, such sediments give rise to soils which are easily rendered infertile. This is why on the floor of the London Basin, particularly in the west around settlements like Camberley, Chobham, and Esher heathland is extensive on the Bagshot Sand and on the dissected veneers of Pleistocene gravel. Smaller heaths also occur on the higher parts of the Chilterns and North Downs, where there are vestiges of Eocene and Plio-Pleistocene sands and gravels. In the Weald, the heathland coincides with the western part of the Lower Greensand outcrop and with the Hastings Beds, which are essentially sandy. As elsewhere in western Europe, the heaths were formerly maintained in a more or less open condition by a regulated pattern of burning and grazing. Now that neither is done systematically reversion to woodland is well advanced, as is obvious from the numerous self-sown trees of birch, pine, oak, and beech.

Expanses of farmland with a great deal of pasture and plentiful oaks, either in scattered woods or in the hedgerows, provide another landscape link between the London Basin and the Weald. By way of contrast, the evidence here suggests wet, cold soils inimical to arable cultivation, and this is exactly what we find. They are formed in the London Clay in the London Basin, and in the Gault Clay and Weald Clay in the Weald. Wherever areas of intensive crop production are encountered they generally signify fertile, loamy soils. River alluvium is widely associated with market gardening, as is the narrow belt of Thanet Sand which separates the Eocene clays from the Chalk along the central and eastern part of the North Downs. Many of the orchards of Kent, incidentally, grow on this deposit and on river alluvium. Finally in this context, the Lower Greensand of Kent has significant reserves of lime and so, unlike its outcrop further west, it too supports excellent farmland and orchards.

With these similarities in mind, it may seem paradoxical that the Chalk hills which surround the London Basin and the Weald display contrasting sequences of vegetation and farmland. The Chilterns carry much beech and oak woodland, whereas on the North Downs similar woodland is confined to the higher ground, above a belt of farmland. In both instances true downland, characterized by short, springy turf and a wealth of flowering herbs, is restricted to the sides of the deeper valleys and to the escarpments. Over the South Downs woodland is scarce and farmland dominates, though real downland is still restricted to slopes in the valleys on the escarpment. Examination of the soil along footpaths and in road cuttings and other excavations soon establishes the reason for these conspicuous scenic differences. The beech and oak woodlands grow on a mantle of very flinty clays overlying the Chalk, and only where they are absent or of limited development is farmland or downland important. In many of the downland localities evidence of change in the landscape is equally plain to see. The rich floral diversity for which the downs are famed resulted from close cropping by sheep and rabbits. With the advent of myxomatosis and intensive farming methods, the grazing pressure has been relaxed enormously to the extent that a massive invasion of thorny scrub and of woodlands of yew, ash, and beech is in progress.

As we have seen, there is often a clear link between soil types and the underlying rocks. However, other factors also contribute to give five widely occurring kinds of soil in the south-east of England and in parts of northern France. These additional factors are: climate, terrain, organisms, and time. Before the spread of prehistoric farmers, soils known as brown earths and their variants were widely developed.

In Fig. 4, the cross-section of an undisturbed brown earth displays a layer or horizon of organic litter (L) on a dark, crumb-structured A layer which is an intimate blend of humus and mineral matter, i.e. mull. Merging out of this is a more coarsely structured B horizon, brown or reddish-brown in colour owing to a lack of humus and which in turn emerges into the parent material (C).

On sandy, gravelly, or granitic parent material more infertile types of brown earth are found, especially where man's influence has been important. Decomposition and the associated cycling of nutrients is slower, and a relatively acid humus known as moder develops. Here the litter layer is succeeded by a fermentation (F) layer and there is less mixing of humus with the mineral soil (Ah). Acids from the moder mobilize iron which passes downwards to a Bs layer. The latter is slightly cemented by iron oxides and has an ochreous hue. Soils with these characteristics are called podzolic

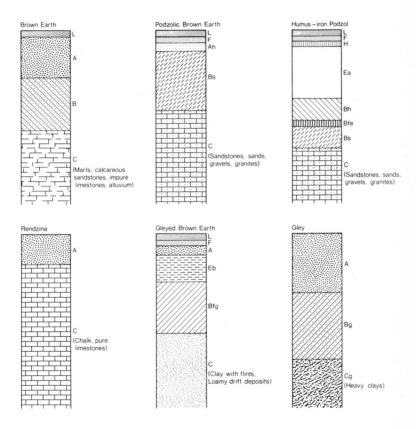

Fig. 4. Some common soil types of north-west Europe. Five factors interact in soil formation, namely parent material, climate, topography, organisms, and time. Before the spread of prehistoric farmers, the brown earth and its variants were the characteristic soils over much of north-west Europe.

brown earths. Further impoverishment of the organic cycles tends to the creation of a very acid mor humus with L, F, and H (humus) horizons. The mor rests sharply on the mineral soil, since the acidity deters earthworms, the main agents in the incorporation of surface organic matter into the soil. Acids from the mor not only mobilize iron but also destroy clay, so that the resultant Ea layer is both structureless and colourless. Below this the iron accumulates to the point where a rusty iron pan (Bfe) is apparent. Organic matter passing through the coarsened Ea horizon is held up on the iron pan and in time a black moor pan (Bh) forms. Such a fully developed sequence is referred to as a humus-iron podzol. In upland environments a more peaty type of podzol is likely to be encountered.

On loamier parent materials in the lowlands brown earths may naturally degrade into gleyed brown earths or *sols lessivés*. Clay particles are washed from the upper part of the soil, leaving a pale, friable Eb layer. The clay particles are deposited in the subsoil and give rise to a blocky structured, brightly coloured Bt horizon. Eventually the build up of clay particles impedes drainage, which causes gleying. This is indicated by the presence of grey streaks and mottles in the clay-enriched zone (Btg).

Superficially these soils resemble the gleys, which are associated with clayey parent materials and are therefore prone to waterlogging. The Bg horizon may be seasonally wet or dry, and so both grey and brown colours prevail. Grey colours usually dominate in the wetter C horizon. As well as clays, chalk and pure limestone also give rise to a distinctive soil type – the rendzina. Since these rocks yield little insoluble residue on weathering, the rendzina is shallow. It comprises an A layer similar in character and appearance to that of the brown earth. There is a sharp junction between the A layer and the underlying chalk or limestone which is due to the effects of solution.

The Straits of Dover

Between Dover and Folkestone the cuesta of the North Downs is cut abruptly by a fine coastline, the eastern section of which provides the famous 'white cliffs'. Comparing the nearly vertical profile of these sea cliffs with the much gentler scarp slope of the North Downs, gives some idea of the undercutting power of the sea. The impression of a retreating coastline is confirmed by two other pieces of evidence. At low tide one can inspect a nearly level wave-cut platform, left behind as the cliffs retreat, and examination of the cliffs themselves reveals that they cut across many ancient valleys, which must once have continued over an area that is now sea.

The floor of the Straits has been studied in some detail. The submarine relief is dominated by a nearly flat plain about 30 m below sea level which cuts across Cretaceous and Jurassic rocks forming the continuation of the Wealden structure. This plain is locally dissected by channels; for example, the Creux de Lobourg, which runs north–south through the eastern half of the Straits and is incised some 30 m into the underlying Chalk. There are also enclosed sediment-filled depressions, such as the narrow Fosse Dangeard. This extends for some 18 km along the Gault Clay outcrop south-east of Dover and its rock floor descends to 120 m below sea level. Elongated sandbanks, trending north-east–south-west, diversify the floor of the Straits. The Varne Bank, which crosses the Fosse Dangeard, is an example. They have been moulded by contemporary currents.

An isthmus may once have extended between Kent and the Boulonnais. The erosional agents that destroyed this land bridge can now only be conjectured, but inferences may be drawn from the submarine relief. One suggestion is that glaciers were directly or indirectly responsible for carving much of the relief of the sea floor during the earlier part of the Ice Age. On this view the submarine plain was eroded by an ice sheet, the enclosed depressions were scoured by meltwater streams beneath the ice, and the Lobourg channel was cut by a separate glacier advancing from the North Sea basin. Intense erosion under cold conditions followed by rising sea levels during the later Ice Age finally completed the destruction of the land bridge. An alternative idea emphasizes the significance of marine processes. This view holds that the submarine floor was planed off by marine erosion, while violent tidal currents scoured and locally overdeepened the network of channels cut by rivers at a time of low sea level. The isthmus was finally destroyed by the combined action of rivers and marine activity. The precise date of this event is unclear but a sudden decrease in the richness of archaeological material in East Anglia at the start of the last interglacial may suggest that the land bridge with France was broken during the previous glacial episode.

Boulonnais

The major structural units of south-east England, the Weald and the London and Hampshire basins, were formed as a result of the great Alpine Earth movements. Their counterparts in northern France, the Pays de Bray and Pas de Calais anticlines, together with the Paris Basin syncline, can also be regarded as 'outer ripples' of the 'Alpine storm'. The formation of these ripples probably culminated between twenty-six and seven million years ago, during the Miocene epoch, when the Mesozoic and younger rocks covering the stable north-west European platform were gently folded. We have already encountered such rocks of Cretaceous and Tertiary age in the London Basin and the Weald; and coal tips in the Betteshanger region of Kent provide evidence of the Palaeozoic 'basement'. Boreholes in this area also demonstrate the presence of Jurassic rocks beneath the Cretaceous and Tertiary formations.

Along the coast between Sangatte and Boulogne and inland towards the village of Licques, both Jurassic and Palaeozoic rocks crop out on the French side of the Channel. The reason for this is the presence of the Boulonnais anticline, which was formed at the same time as the Weald. The subsequent erosion of this structure has exposed the older strata. Short visits to the coast and inland are enough to demonstrate a remarkable number of geological phenomena within a limited area, and will provide a suitable introduction to the more complex regions of the Jura and the Alps. In view of the interest of this area to the geologist the following account is rather more extended than those for other localities *en route*.

Numerous accessible coastal sections provide opportunities for conducting detailed studies of both Cretaceous and Jurassic strata, for collecting fossils, and for interpreting the conditions that prevailed at the time when these beds were deposited. At Sangatte the Middle Chalk crops out at beach level, and careful collection will yield fossils similar to those from the rocks of corresponding age on the English side of the Channel. These include echinoids and brachiopods. Unfortunately the Upper Chalk is poorly exposed in the Boulonnais and there are few opportunities, except from limited outcrops, of collecting the various echinoids or crinoids used as zone fossils. They include *Micraster* (Fig. 5) and *Marsupites* which are fairly common in the cliffs between Dover and Ramsgate.

Just south-west of Sangatte there is evidence of relatively recent changes in both sea-level and climate. Examination of the cliff face near the old Channel Tunnel workings reveals a section through an old cliff line, which now trends inland and is clearly displayed south of the road to Coquelles. To the north of this ancient cliff is a pasty deposit, the Coombe Rock, which was laid down under very cold, arctic conditions during the last Ice Age. This rests on a raised platform, mantled with beach shingle, which indicates that sea-level was higher than it is now.

The dip of the beds near Sangatte is generally to the north-east and the indication is that to the south-west one should encounter older strata in the descent of the stratigraphic column. This is borne out on the beach below the cliffs of Petit Blanc Nez where slumped masses of Gault Clay, similar to that exposed in the Vale of Holmesdale at Westerham, cover the foreshore, The Gault underlies the Lower Chalk, and it is possible to collect various clams, gastropods, ammonites, and fish teeth from this fine-grained, essentially deep-water sediment. Unlike the Chalk, it is difficult to recognize individual layers or beds within the tenacious, rather featureless Gault because no distinct layers of flints occur to help identify dip and strike. Sands and clays, the approximate time equivalents of the Lower Greensand and Wealden, succeed the Gault along the coast towards Wissant.

At Cap Gris Nez (Fig. 2) the Cretaceous rocks give way to those of Jurassic age with a coarse-grained, resistant sandstone (the Grès de la Crêche) capping older clays (the Argiles de Chatillon). (Both sandstones and clays are termed clastic rocks which mean that they are the products of erosion.) The sandstones (Plate 2) cropping out along this stretch of coast, including the Grès de la Crêche, provide a wealth of information on past environments of deposition, and it is possible to examine cross-bedding and ripple marks similar to those formed today under shallow-water conditions. Body fossils such as clams and gastropods are fairly common, as are trace fossils which reflect the burrowing activities of worms and various arthropods. Such traces are extremely useful in determining the depth of deposition and in establishing the level of energy that prevailed within the marine environ-

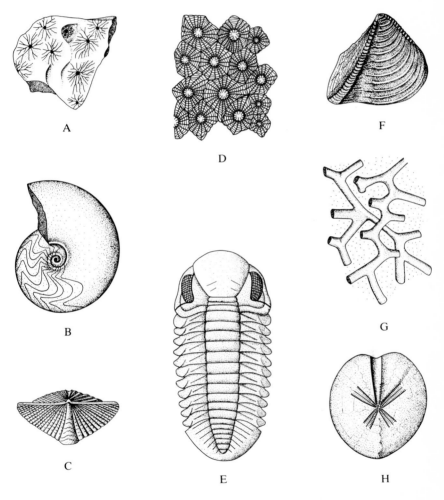

Fig. 5. Some fossils from the rocks of Kent and northern France. Diagrams A–E show fossils from the Palaeozoic rocks of the Ferques inlier, F–G fossils from the Jurassic rocks of the Boulonnais, and H an echinoid from the Chalk of Kent. (A) Stromatoporoid; (B) *Hexagonaria*, a coral; (C) a spiriferid brachiopod; (D) *Manticoceras*, a goniatite; (E) *Phacops*, a trilobite; (F) *Trigonia*, a bivalve; (G) Trace fossil, *Thalassinoides*; (H) *Micraster*.

ment. In general terms, vertical, simple burrows are characteristic of shoreline and shallow-water environments, while oblique and horizontal burrows, showing increasing complexity, suggest deeper waters. In the Boulonnais trace fossils have been used to reconstruct a detailed model of the conditions that existed at the time of deposition.

Sandstones and clays are not the only sediments exposed in this region, and a number of limestones can be identified. The latter are mostly associated with shallow shelf seas that do not receive much fragmentary, or clastic, materials (sand, silts, clays). Such seas are also characterized by a high production of organic skeletal material, from which the carbonate minerals may be derived. The production of carbonates is greatest in warm-water regions, and limestones containing abundant algal, bivalve, and coral fossils may imply warm, temperate to subtropical conditions. In the Boulonnais most of the Jurassic carbonate rocks are impure, with a high sand or clay fraction, which suggests that they were probably deposited close to an ancient shoreline. The degree of fragmentation of the enclosed skeletal materials also serves as an indicator of energy levels. Inland, Jurassic limestones older than those exposed along the coast can be seen to have been formed by the accumulation of small carbonate spheres called ooids. At the present day limestones of this type are being formed in the very shallow waters that surround the atolls of the Caribbean.

Apart from the wealth of information they provide on Jurassic environments and ancient communities, the Sangatte – Boulogne sections also provide important clues to the overall structure of the region. At La Crèche (Fig. 2), a few kilometres north of Boulogne, the oldest Jurassic rocks exposed on the coast are brought to the surface in the core of the Crèche anticline. So far on our journey we have been able to deduce the structures of the major folds of the Weald and London Basin only from dip and strike evidence, but here we can observe an obvious flexure in the Earth's crust. Note that the Crèche anticline is asymmetrical with the steeper dips occurring on the northern limb. The axis of the fold trends north-west – south-east. A few hundred metres beyond the axis of the anticline, to the north, a well-defined fault can be seen in the cliff face.

The Jurassic rocks exposed along the coast were deposited in the later half of that period; outcrops of earlier Jurassic rocks are known only from boreholes or inland where they cap rocks of the Palaeozoic core. The unconformable junction between the Jurassic and Palaeozoic rocks of the region is exposed in several quarries on the northern limbs of the main Boulonnais–Artois anticline. The Palaeozoic rocks were brought towards the surface as a result of various structural events and exposed by erosion. The area of exposure is referred to as the Ferques inlier (Fig. 6), a term which aptly describes the fact that the Palaeozoic rocks here are completely surrounded by rocks of younger age. The Palaeozoic sediments within the inlier are mostly of Devonian and Carboniferous ages, although irrefutable evidence of the presence of Silurian shales has come from borehole cores containing the graptolite *Monograptus colonus*.

These fine-grained shales were deposited under deep-water conditions, which contrast with the shallow-water environment postulated for the pebble beds and sandstones that mark the advance of the Devonian seas across the area. In the various quarries it is posible to examine excellent exposures of the limestones and shales that succeeded the basal deposits and to collect numerous representatives of various groups of invertebrates. Among the most significant of these are the remains of stromatoporoids and hexagonarid corals (Fig. 5), which are closely related to the living *Hydra* and sea anemones, together with brachiopods, goniatites, and trilobites. In some quarries sufficient evidence exists for the palaeontologist to reconstruct the reef communities that flourished here over 350 million years ago.

Limestones also form a major part of the Carboniferous succession in the area and, although brachiopods and corals persist as important components of the fossil community, it is possible to recognize that major replacements have taken place at genetic and species levels. These changes are important to the palaeontologist and stratigrapher because they enable them to date and correlate strata from different areas. This technique may be used for the youngest Carboniferous rocks of the Ferques inlier, because the remains of Coal Measure plants from the tip-heaps of former mines are identical to those from the Kent and northern France coal fields.

In the quarries of the Ferques inlier numerous faults and limited, but fairly complex, folding can be seen, which provide evidence of Earth movements. The overlying Jurassic rocks are unaffected (Fig. 6) and we can readily assume that these structural features are, therefore, the product of the post-Carboniferous, Hercynian orogeny. The quarries themselves are evidence of the exploitation of natural resources; the various limestones rank among the most important facing and ornamental stones of France.

We have now established that the general structure of the Boulonnais is similar to that of the Weald, and one might expect that the scenery should also be comparable. However, there are some important differences between the landscapes of these two regions. A striking contrast is that of scale. A central vantage point hardly reveals the unity of the Wealden landscape for the Downs are too remote, but from most of the escarpments rimming the Bas-Boulonnais the central eroded core of the anticline is clearly seen, and offers a fine illustration of inverted relief. One can see the work done by erosional agents even more clearly from the central hill of Mont Lambert (188 metres), which lies just east of Boulogne.

A second important difference between the two landscapes is apparent looking out over the Bas-Boulonnais. Its central region does not show the clear development of cuestas that are so typical of the Weald. It is difficult to understand the reasons for this from a study of the present landscape, and we have to rely on geological evidence and theoretical ideas, as is quite often

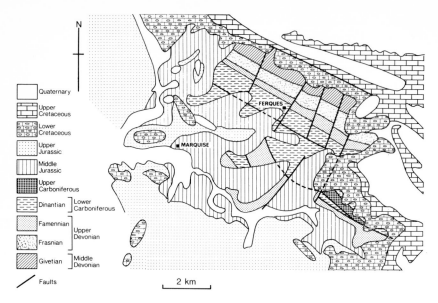

Fig. 6(a). A geological map of the Ferques inlier showing a faulted and essentially gently folded sequence of Palaeozoic rocks surrounded by sediments of Mesozoic age.

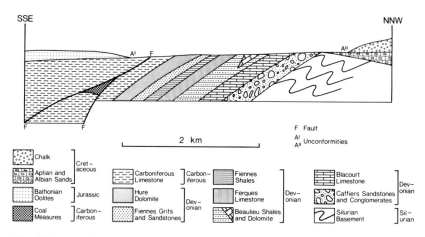

Fig. 6(b). A section across the Ferques inlier showing the general dip of the Palaeozoic rocks and the unconformable boundary between them and the overlying Jurassic and Cretaceous deposits.

the case in studies of scenery. First, the most recent episode of erosion which exposed the present depression followed earlier episodes which had removed much of the most resistant rock. Secondly, pre-Cretaceous earth movements had so dislocated resistant strata that no extensive areas could emerge as upstanding relief. A third factor is the nearness of the sea, which enhanced the rate at which streams carried out erosion in the Boulonnais depression.

In Bas-Boulonnais the range and character of the farmland and vegetation inevitably resemble that of the Weald, because the same fundamental geological controls are present. The sandstones are co-extensive with heath-like scenery, the clays support pasture and small woods, and the limestones carry much downland.

From Ferques one can rejoin the main road to Arras by travelling via the village of Guines. This short cross-country route avoids returning to Calais, and instead goes across the contact between Palaeozoic and Mesozoic strata and then on to the undulating countryside of the Upper Chalk. The St. Omer–Reims route (Fig. 7) essentially follows the eastern margin of the Paris Basin, with the great coal tips of the Béthune region serving as a reminder of the Palaeozoic basement, and of the general continuity of the regions we have journeyed across.

We have now returned to the Chalk outcrop. Indeed, the journey from the Boulonnais towards Laon is almost entirely on Chalk, and provides many opportunities for examining the distinctive scenery developed on this rock and for comparing it with that of the downlands of south-east England.

A French geographer (P. Pinchemel in *Les Plaines de Craie*, p. 21 (1954)) has described the scenery of Picardy as

calm, monotonous yet harmonious, with no particular reference point, and giving the traveller the impression of an endless canvas on which the same panorama recurs: extensive plateaux or plains, modified by depressions or by the green ribbon of a valley floor. Everywhere the convex slopes give a certain amplitude and serenity to the landscape. There are no abrupt changes or dramatic contrasts.

Compare this description with the English Downs.

More prosaic investigations have revealed the circumstances under which the scenery of Artois and Picardy has been developed, and the reasons for the similarities and contrasts with the English Downs. You can confirm many of the lines of argument for yourself. An examination of the residual deposits resting on the Chalk (Plate 3) typically reveals, in addition to whitened flints in various stages of destruction, deposits of blackened and rounded pebbles together with sandstone fragments. A roadside exposure about 9 kilometres west of St Quentin on route N44 shows the character of these superficial materials, and at the same time reveals the way in which they are piped into the underlying chalk. In Artois sands of Eocene age have locally buried an ancient, irregular Chalk landscape. The evidence of these deposits suggests that the Chalk surface was roughed out during post-

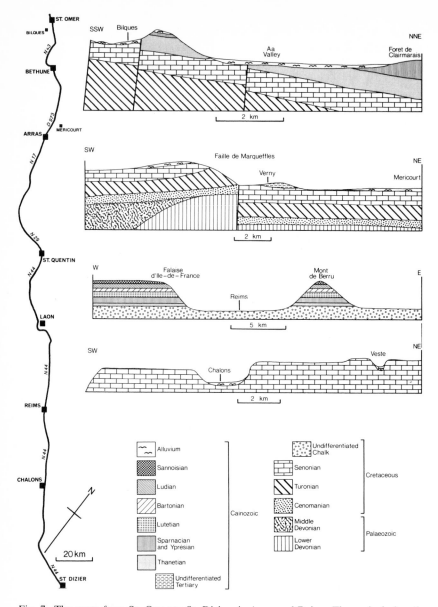

Fig. 7. The route from St. Omer to St. Dizier via Arras and Reims. The geological sections contrast with those of the gently folded structures of London Basin and the Weald, and of the complex structures of the Alps.

18

Cretaceous times, buried by Tertiary sediments, and subsequently exhumed. Some details of its present form are partly due to geological structures. The strategic barrier of the Vimy ridge (130 metres to 160 metres high) north of Arras is associated with the faulted anticline of the Artois axis, and the ridge of high ground (up to 128 metres) north-west of St Quentin which separates the Somme and Escaut river systems, is developed on the Artois anticline. West of St Quentin extends the nearly flat Santerre plain, whose valleys are incised only a few metres below its general level. The surface of this plain coincides with the bedding of the Chalk, which is here almost horizontal.

The extensive network of dry valleys that incise the Chalk may have been carved by streams established on the cover of Tertiary rocks. Most of their discharge may have been lost when they cut into the underlying permeable Chalk. An alternative view, already discussed for some of the dry valleys of the North Downs, suggests that surface streams actively eroded the Chalk during glacial periods when the ground was largely frozen and so impermeable. On this view the gently rounded land surface was moulded by the combined action of frost and water.

By the time you approach Laon you will be able to appreciate the reasons for the similarities and contrasts in scenery between French and English chalklands. A family resemblance is expressed in the dry valley systems and by the smoothly rounded slopes, while the wide panoramas of Picardy, hardly matched by the North Downs, result from a much greater area occupied by Chalk.

The importance of whether or not the soil is actually formed in the Chalk or in a superficial cover of other material, is well seen in the country between Calais and Reims. Although morphologically alike, the three subregions which make up this northern part of France, namely Artois, Picardy, and Dry Champagne, have rather different rural identities. In Artois, the not uncommon presence of surface water, together with impressive areas of cereals, sugar beet, and fodder crops, show that the Chalk is not the dominant soil parent material, for chalk-derived soils are very shallow and dry. In fact, there is a considerable covering of a loamy deposit known as *limon*, which is the reworked waste of a former wind-blown sediment, or loess, laid down in the glacial phases of the Pleistocene. Picardy, too, has a mantle of *limon*, but there are also patches of flinty clay and, because many of these are under woodland or scrub, the landscape is more varied. Added diversification is provided by the larger alluvial-floored valleys, where there is intensive market gardening, that of the Somme supplying the Amiens markets. The Dry Champagne, in contrast, has a more deserted, monotonous aspect, for here the *limon* covering is almost entirely lacking. Traditionally, the dry, dusty soils supported a meagre population heavily dependent upon sheep grazing. Only in the last fifty years or so has a more prosperous mixed farming economy emerged, as a result of a programme of heavy fertilization and general agricultural reorganization.

19

Although most of the chalkland of northern France has experienced agrarian reform in recent decades one very distinctive feature of the rural scene has endured, namely the open, uninterrupted aspect of the cultivated areas. The general absence of hedges and permanent field boundaries is inherited from a way of life formerly prevalent not only in this part of France, but also in other parts of north-west Europe, including lowland Britain. Farms were then smaller, more numerous and occurred in nuclear groupings from which many of the present-day villages are descended. Typically, the ploughland around these settlements was arranged into three vast fields, each of which was left fallow every third year. The fields were subdivided into long strips, and an individual farmer held several strips scattered over the three fields. Livestock, on the other hand, were kept in communal herds and flocks. To obtain enough grazing for the flocks, it was vital that the various strips being left fallow should all have been thrown open to the animals at the same time. This meant that the farmers in each settlement had to follow a common cycle of ploughing, seeding, and harvesting. Hence, while the strips were suited to individual husbandry, they were necessarily amalgamated for communal use; stock-proof boundaries such as hedges were clearly inappropriate. In Britain the open fields have long been enclosed by hedgerows; indeed the transformation was far advanced in the eighteenth century. Evidently agriculture in northern France developed along different lines, yet the old strip system of cultivation from which the contemporary open vistas have evolved has been obliterated just as effectively. This was achieved by a systematic regrouping and enlargement of individual land holdings, particularly since 1945, aimed at a highly intensive, mechanized, agricultural industry.

The name Champagne, incidentally, signifies an open-field landscape, while in English the term champion is similarly associated with open, rolling country. It is worth noting, however, that the vineyards which produce the famous champagne grapes do not grow in this kind of setting. They are concentrated instead along an east-facing limestone escarpment overlooking the Chalk. This escarpment marks the boundary of the Île de France – the outcrop of Tertiary rocks occupying the centre of the Paris Basin.

South-east of La Fère the route climbs steadily away from the valley of the Oise and passes over gently undulating Chalk scenery. After some 20 kilometres the town of Laon comes into view, impressively perched on a large, isolated hill whose origin invites speculation. Closer examination reveals that the hill is capped by a resistant limestone that overlies sands of lower Eocene age. The view to the south and south-west, best seen from the tourist circuit of the ramparts, reveals the escarpments of the Île de France. and you can easily see how its form varies between straight and serrated. The hill on which Laon stands is a remnant left behind by the irregular retreat of this escarpment, and is called a butte. As it is flat-topped the term mesa may also be used, but this term is normally restricted to the larger examples. You have yet to confirm the Tertiary age of the escarpment, and so its former continuity with the butte, but this theme will be developed further for the vicinity of Reims. Meanwhile, as you drive from Laon, note the Tertiary promontory of Festieux with its associated buttes.

Reims – the Dry Champagne

For many tourists the city of Reims and its cathedral are obvious attractions, and warrant an overnight stop. The city is also attractive in that it is the capital town of the Dry Champagne, or Champagne pouilleuse, region, and for those who are interested in both wine and the Earth Sciences it is ideally situated for a study of the eastern margin of the Paris Basin.

The city straddles the River Vesle, and is built on the Chalk of the 'plaine de Champagne'. Excellent views of this fertile region may be obtained from several high localities just to the north-east of the city, and from a good vantage point you may observe the high ground of the Falaise de l'Île de France to the west, and that of Mont Berru to the east. These two landscape units provide significant items of evidence for the way in which the scenery has evolved.

The visible portion of the Falaise de l'Île is part of a long-dissected cuesta, whose escarpment defines the eastern rim of the Île de France, the central core of the Paris Basin. The steep scarp slope in the vicinity of Reims is developed across Tertiary limestones and Chalk. The escarpment is highly indented by comparison with the much straighter appearance of, for example, the North Downs. The explanation for this serrated outline lies partly in the work done by a number of closely-spaced streams, including the Aisne, Vesle, and Marne, which cut through the cuesta during their journey to the west. As a result, the plan form of the cuesta turns sharply westward where the streams meet the line of the escarpment. The streams occupy quite impressive valleys: that of the Marne west of Epernay is remarkably narrow and steep walled.

The high ground of Mont Berru (267 metres) (Fig. 7) provides further evidence of the way in which the relief has developed. This upland is also made of Tertiary rocks, and a bed-by-bed comparison with the Falaise de l'Île reveals that they were once part of the same geological unit. This evidence demonstrates that a great deal of erosion has taken place, involving the removal of virtually all the Tertiary beds that once extended westwards to the Falaise. Mont Berru is a fine example of an outlier, which in this instance also forms a butte, an upland left behind by the irregular retreat of the Falaise escarpment. The high ground of the Montagne de Reims, 12 kilometres south of the city, has also been left behind by the relatively rapid retreat of the escarpment to both north and south, and now forms an imposing eastward pointing promontory. In due course it also will become a butte.

At the top of Mont Berru it is possible to obtain one of the best views of the Champagne district; its open fields, blocks of pine plantations, and vineyards on the scarp of the Falaise de l'Île. Various sections between the village of Berru and the summit demonstrate both the nature of the contact between the Chalk and the overlying Tertiaries, and the character of the various Tertiary sands and clays. As in the London Basin the junction is unconformable, and here again no marked change in angularity is apparent. The unconformity stands well above the level of the surrounding Chalk plains. This suggests that the surface of the Dry Champagne has been lowered by erosion while the Falaise escarpment was retreating. The Tertiaries of Mont Berru have therefore protected the underlying Chalk. The majority of sediments on Mont Berru were deposited under essentially continental conditions. Although you can observe some sedimentary features and collect a limited variety of fossils here, you will get a truer impression of the conditions that existed in the Paris Basin during the Tertiary by visiting localities to the east or south of Reims.

One excursion in particular, to the Montagne de Reims, is well worth while. Apart from investigating the geology and scenery, one can see some of the more reputable vineyards of this famous region. This excursion, like all others, should be planned with the aid of regional guides, such as those listed in the bibliography, but the villages of Rilly, Verzenay, and Verzy are classic stopping points. At Rilly it is possible to see again the junction between the Chalk and Tertiaries and to collect fossils from the lacustrine sands which are of Thanetian age. Near Verzenay and Verzy more complete sections through the Tertiaries show sediments that span some twenty million years of geological time. Abundant fossils from various levels indicate both marine and lacustrine environments. For example, a sequence of marls near the top of both sections yields numerous echinoids, clams, and gastropods, These marls were deposited during the Ludian stage of the Tertiary period, and they probably mark the most easterly advance of the seas during that time. Only a visit to the enormous Lambert Quarries at Cormeilles en Parisis, to the west of Paris, could provide a more rewarding review of Tertiary stratigraphy than a visit to the outcrops of Rilly, Verzenay, and Verzy.

The plateau surface of the Montagne throws further light on the development of the scenery. The high ground is dissected by a series of valleys, those near Vaurémont, for example, are characterized by smooth, debris-mantled slopes and gentle, long profiles. The gradients suddenly steepen as they descend to join a major stream, usually the Marne. The upper sections of these valleys originally declined smoothly to join an ancestral Marne, then flowing well above its present course. These are ancient, suspended valleys, which were in existence well before the Ice Age, and are among the oldest features of the present landscape. Such evidence is of great value in studies of the evolution of scenery.

The undulating landscape of the Dry Champagne is cut by a number of streams, including the Aisne and the Marne, which are part of a larger network focusing on the Seine. Their valleys through the Chalk repay investigation. The first point to notice is that these streams do flow: chalk is a highly permeable rock, and normally does not carry a surface flow. These rivers have, however, sealed their beds with a layer of water-borne sediment or alluvium, so they are effectively flowing on impermeable rock. The second point of note is the relatively large size of the valleys, which appear far too big for the volumes of water they are carrying. Such oversized valleys – called misfits – are a result of conditions at the close of the Ice Age when much greater volumes of run-off were available and carved large valleys. (This is a common theme in western Europe.) A third point of interest is the nature of the river channels themselves. In some cases the flood plain has been incised by several channels which between them carry the flow. This type of channel pattern is called braided, and may in this area have resulted from a reduction in discharge. Elsewhere the channel pattern shows a development of tight sinuous curves or meanders, which are well displayed south-west of La Fère and in the valley of the Marne north-west of Châlons. This pattern normally develops where streams flow on gentle gradients across fine alluvium.

Near Châlons, the Marne, rather like the Thames, shows evidence of a complicated Ice Age history. A system of low terraces (Fig. 8) may be seen, notably between Fagnières and St Martin. Detailed investigation by earth scientists has revealed that the deposits of the highest and lowest terraces are largely made up of chalk debris (called *grève* in Champagne, and similar in origin to the English coombe rock), while the intermediate terrace consists of sand and clays laid down in a much milder period. Terraces and their constituents provide much information for unravelling a river's history.

Châlons-sur-Marne to Langres

South of Reims the Dry Champagne region forms a distinct aureole around the Tertiaries of the Paris Basin. Route N44 finally crosses the margin or rim

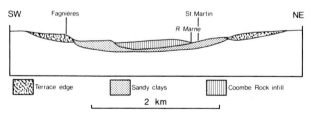

Fig. 8. Terraces of the Marne near Châlons. A sheet of cold climate chalky debris (*grève* or coombe rock) has been dissected to form a 'terrace edge'. The valley was then partly filled by sandy clays during warmer interglacial conditions, shallowly dissected, and, finally, a further narrow sheet of *grève* was laid down.

of the underlying Chalk near Vitry le François, where the Falaise de Champagne forms a pronounced escarpment, facing eastward, and showing that it is still in the geological province of the Paris Basin. The descent from the Chalk, together with a significant change in vegetation and drainage, marks the transition to the 'Champagne humide' or Wet Champagne district. Unlike the dry plains of the Chalk this region is poorly drained. There are many shallow lakes and marshy depressions, such as the Lac du Der Chantecoq, south-west of St Dizier. There has been much clearance and draining during historic times, and it is clear that this must originally have been an area of extensive swamps, lakes, and forests. All this evidence suggests that the underlying rock is soft and impermeable; it is in fact the Gault Clay.

The soft nature of the Gault, together with its poor drainage qualities, imply that it is readily attacked by river action. The most obvious result has been the development of a strike vale, so called because it follows the strike of the Gault. A less obvious result, which affects the pattern of stream courses, may be studied from a map. Examine the course of the River Ornain, which flows east of the Marne and parallel to it as far as Bar le Duc. At that town the Ornain swings abruptly west, and joins the Marne near Vitry le François. The explanation for this unusual arrangement is that a tributary of the Marne, joining at Vitry, worked its way headward across the easily eroded Gault until it met the line of the Ornain, which was then diverted or 'captured' by the energetic tributary. The ancient course of the Ornain, revealed by a ribbon of river debris, can be traced north to Ste Menehould. This process of river capture is quite common in areas made up of alternating soft and hard rocks, such as the Weald and the Paris Basin, and should always be borne in mind as an explanation for sudden changes in a stream's direction.

There are some significant differences between the landscape of the Champagne humide and that developed on the same formation in the Weald. The surface of the Wet Champagne is more undulating, with enough drainage on the higher ground to permit arable cultivation and the establishment of orchards on southern slopes. River alluvium and residuals of Upper Greensand rocks in all stages of demolition are also scattered across the Gault, and are picked out by areas of mixed farmland or heathland.

On our chosen route the main outcrop of the poorly exposed Gault ends just south of St Dizier, where after a few kilometres Cretaceous rocks give way to the limestones of the Plateau des Bars. These rocks, like those between Cap Gris Nez and Boulogne, were deposited in the upper part of the Jurassic period and may be regarded as the equivalents of the Portlandian of Dorset. The regional dip of this formation is towards the north-west. The limestones of the Plateau des Bars (Fig. 9) in turn cap the Kimmeridge Clay. South of St Dizier the road follows the valley of the Marne, which becomes steadily more pronounced as it cuts down into the limestone of the plateau.

The gentle gradients of the valley floor contrast with the steep wooded slopes above and with the nearly flat skyline of the plateau. The highly irregular scarp slope of the Bars cuesta at Joinville overlooks the Kimmeridge Clay Vale. The surface of the northern edge of the vale is veneered with rock debris, whose nature shows that it has been eroded from the limestone escarpment. This evidence provides confirmation of the reality of scarp retreat, and of the way in which cuestas evolve. About 20 kilometres south of Joinville a roadside cutting reveals the deeply weathered limestone surface, with a complicated unit of superficial deposits, some of which were laid down during the Ice Age.

The alternation of limestone and clay which constitute the area of the Plateau des Bars corresponds, predictably enough, with a regular variation of land use. A mosaic of rough grazing and woodland typifies the higher parts of the limestones, giving way to ploughed land on the deeper soils of the gentler lower slopes. The belt of Kimmeridge Clay is associated with dairy and beef pastures. Because of the combination of south-east aspect, dry soils, and long hours of sunshine in late summer and early autumn, numerous vineyards have been laid out on the limestone hillsides. The wine they produce is placed in the Burgundy category. The narrow outcrop of Kimmeridge Clay supports the famous vineyards of Chablis.

Beyond the Kimmeridgian the road cuts through the gentle dip slope of the Oxfordian, a series of calcareous marlstones and limestones that eventually form a further distinct cuesta twelve kilometres north of Chaumont. This town is sited on the flank of the valley of the Marne, which here incises the limestone escarpment. A local summit, the Côte d'Alun (384 metres), offers fine views both beyond and along the cuesta, and it is possible to see the depression of La Vallée at the foot of the scarp, and also the broad landscape of the Langres–Chatillonais plateau to the south. The depression is a further example of a strike vale, developed on the outcrop of weakly resistant marls and calcareous marls of Oxfordian and Callovian age. The plateau beyond is formed of Callovian and Bathonian limestones.

Nearer to Chaumont it is possible to visit several local quarries on the plateau. These are on the main Paris road a few hundred metres beyond the Paris–St Dizier–Chaumont crossroads.

The first quarry, on the south side of the road, is cut into the compact grey–white limestones of the Upper Bathonian, and various levels yield numerous fossils, including the important brachiopod *Rhynchonella decorata*. Other fossils include gastropods, bivalves, and algal oncoliths. The latter are mostly rounded and in cross-section are composed of numerous laminations, each of which represents the former surface of an algal ball that once literally rolled around in the tidal zone of the warm Middle Jurassic seas accreting fine sediment. In many parts of this quarry the limestones are shot with the distinctive traces of stylolites, irregular lines which are the result of pressure solution. Further along the road quarries on both sides contain

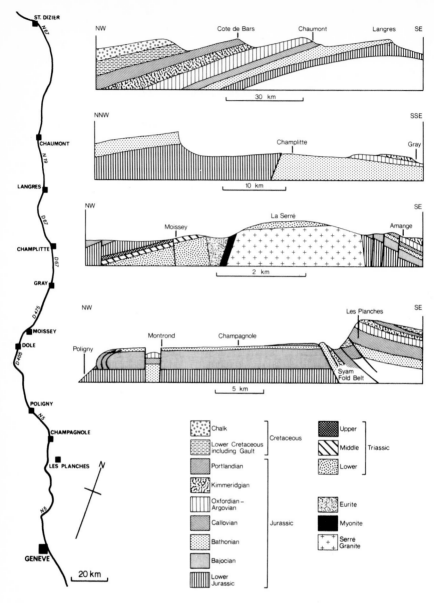

Fig. 9. Route map from St. Dizier to Geneva via Langres and Les Planches. The geological sections illustrate the form of the northern cuestas, the faulted junction between the Liassic plain below Langres and the Plateau de la Haute Saône, the structure of the Serre Massif, and fault-dissected plateau beyond Poligny.

26

exposures of the uppermost Bathonian. Again the sediments are limestones but in both quarries they are oolitic with various levels exhibiting excellent cross-stratification. In the northernmost Daverio quarry the Bathonian limestones are capped by calcareous marls of Callovian age which contain fossils of ammonites (*Macrocephalites*) and brachiopods (*Digonella*).

Beyond Chaumont, road sections and other outcrops on the Langres Plateau (Fig. 9) indicate that the regional dip is again towards the north-west. Therefore, travelling southwards, we are steadily descending the stratigraphic column, passing over the Callovian and Bathonian on to limestones of the Bajocian, or Lower Middle Jurassic. South of Rolampont the Marne valley opens out, and fine views of the walled town of Langres, perched on the irregular and dissected scarp of the limestone cuesta, can be obtained. A good vantage point is La Roche de Charmes, about 8 kilometres north of Langres. From the plain below Langres, it is possible to observe not only the low angle of the dip slope, but also the thickness of the limestones that overlie the Liassic clays and marls of the plain. The limestones of the Langres plateau are predominantly oolitic in character, with local concentrations of bryozoans and corals.

The pattern of land use on the Plateau de Langres is similar to that developed in the area of the Plateau de Bars. Woodlands of beech, oak, and chestnut, conifer plantantions, and scrubby grassland account for much of the oolitic limestone outcrop, not least in the highest localities where rainfall is quite heavy. Rich pasture and mixed farmland in the major river valleys, on the other hand, are evidence of the removal by erosion of the limestone, thereby exposing the underlying Lias clays and marls. Again, vineyards are concentrated on to the south-east-facing escarpment of the plateau, where rainfall is lower and the hours of sunshine longer.

Langres to Geneva

From Langres the preferred route to Switzerland is via Gray, Dôle, Champagnole, and Morez. This avoids many major towns and crosses most of the structural units of the Jura. The Plateau de Langres reaches a maximum height of some 650 metres and then falls away abruptly to the south. As the road descends the escarpment and crosses the Marne–Saône canal the fine limestone outlier of Grigol comes into view away to the east, rising abruptly from the Liassic clay plain. This butte has been left behind by the retreat of the escarpment.

Between Langres and Gray, the outcrop of the Lias is broken by residual limestone units which give rise to upstanding relief features. To the south the boundary between Lias and the plateau limestones is marked by a major fault, trending north-east–south-west and forming an obvious north-facing slope approximately 12 kilometres to the north of the village of Champlitte. Roadside exposures reveal that the limestones are of Middle and Upper

Jurassic age and that the regional dip, south of the fault, is to the south-south-east. In the vicinity of Gray terrace fragments represent ancient flood plains of the Saône. The Saône itself is prone to flooding, and this may affect the lowest terraces, as well as the flood plain. Beyond Gray, to the south of the River Ognon, the southern margin of the plateau is again fault-bounded. From Gray to Dôle the road skirts the boundary between the Plateaux de la Haute-Saône and the Bresse Graben, a downfaulted trough which lies to the south-west.

This graben is one of the major structural units of the southern pre-Jura region. It was downfaulted during the early Tertiary and subsequently infilled with deposits of marine and terrestrial origin. The boundary between the northern plateau and the downfaulted unit does not follow a straight line; northern extensions of the graben are crossed south of both Gray and Dôle (Forêt de Chaux), respectively.

The southern faulted boundary of the Plateaux de la Haute-Saône is a low-angled thrust, the rocks of the much-faulted Avant Monts Zone being pushed over those of the plateaux. Direct contact between the two blocks corresponds roughly with the southern scarp of the Ognon valley and extends for approximately 60 kilometres towards the north-east. Somewhat unexpectedly the southern region of the thrust zone, around the village of Montmirey, is more complex than the main fault line to the north, with the small Massif de la Serre rising above the plains of the Saône. Geographically, the Serre Massif is a small feature, but its relevance to the geological history of the region and even to that of Europe is considerable. On the Montagne de la Serre (Fig. 9) itself, we stand, for the first time during the journey, on the true foundations of the continent, with rocks of the Pre-Cambrian basement being uplifted by faulting. Structurally the Massif is known as a horst, a fault-bounded block which has been raised up relative to the surrounding younger strata. The rocks of the Massif are metamorphic: they have been altered by the forces of several major phases of mountain-building and by the intrusion of igneous rocks, such as granites, during the Hercynian orogeny. They are gneisses: coarse grained rocks with an abundance of quartz and an irregular and discontinuous banding. A short detour off the N475 just south of Montmirey, east to the village of Offlanges and the large Moissey quarry, takes you across the Jurassic on to Permo-Triassic rocks and contact with the crystalline basement.

The scenery of the massif shows a repetitive contrast between forested ridges and cultivated lower slopes and valley floors. The soils contrast with the more fertile areas of the Avant Monts and the Forêt de Chaux which are lime-rich and generally more clayey. The Avants Monts plateau and a series of pre-Jura hills are composed of Jurassic rocks thrust northward. These rocks were also folded and faulted during the Alpine Orogeny. In the region of Besançon the rocks of the plateaux are faulted directly against the much-folded and faulted strata of the Ledonian–Bisontin arc, a region not en-

countered on the route until you have crossed over the Tertiary rocks
preserved in the northern extension of the Bresse Graben, referred to above
as the Forêt de Chaux. South of Dôle the road crosses the wide and
complicated flood plains of the rivers Doubs and Loue. The landscape
details are difficult to grasp from the roadside, but the 1/100 000 topographic
map is useful for an appreciation of the varying channel patterns made by
these rivers.

The rocks of the Ledonian–Bisontin Arc form a distinct break in slope
across the N5, some 12 kilometres north of Poligny. This marks the faulted
junction between the Tertiaries and Jurassic rocks of the arc, with thrusting
taking the older series over the younger. Because the younger rocks have
remained *in situ*, as have the basement rocks over which the Jurassics were
also thrust, they are termed autochthonous, as opposed to allochthonous for
the thrusted materials. The Ledonian–Bisontin Arc, the folded outer edge
of the external Jura, passes south-south-eastwards in the Plateau de Lons le
Saunier. The village of Poligny (Fig. 9) lies at the foot of this plateau. South
of the town, towards Champagnole, the N5 winds steadily up a most spectacular scarp slope via the large dry valley known as the Reculée de Vaux.
From Poligny to the scarp the route climbs from the clays of the Lias on to
the oolitic limestones of the Middle Jurassic that underlie the Plateau de
Lons le Saunier. This almost monotonous, forested landscape shows the dry
valleys, closed depressions, irregular surfaces, and rocky outcrops diagnostic
of a hard limestone. The plateau surface is a fragment of a formerly more
extensive feature that resulted from a lengthy period of erosion under a
warm, dry climate during the late Tertiary times. An erosion surface cut
under these conditions is called a pediplain.

The Reculée de Vaux and the Cirque du Fer à Cheval (Plate 4) are two of a
number of interesting valleys that cut into the surface of the ancient
pediplain. A short diversion northwards along the N469 leads to a fine
vantage point, the Belvedere de la Chatelaine, which overlooks a further
spectacular dry valley, the Reculée des Planches. The heads of these valleys
are steep, almost cliff-like (they are called *bouts de monde*), and most of
them have a spring or grotto at their base. They provide important evidence
for landscape development after the fashioning of the main pediplain. They
are all found at the lower sections of dry valleys, and appear to have
developed by a combination of solution and joint-controlled collapse of the
limestone, as subterranean stream systems steadily cut into the rock. The
action of frost maintained the cliff-like character of the valley heads.

Near Montrond the road crosses the 'chaine de l'Euthe' (Fig. 9), which is
expressed scenically as a depression. Structurally it is a graben, floored by
Oxford Clay. At Montrond the chateau sits on limestones of the Upper
Jurassic which in turn rest upon the Oxford Clay. The rocks of the Plateau de
Lons that form the cliffs to the north are older. The Plateau de Lons to the
north, and the Plateau de Champagnole to the south, are part of a formerly

continuous land surface that was subsequently broken by movement along the chaine de l'Euthe.

Towards the south-east the Tertiary pediplain is well displayed as the Plateau de Champagnole, developed across rocks of middle Jurassic age. In the vicinity of Champagnole itself there is good evidence for the existence of a second, higher-level pediplain, the Nozeroy surface, standing at about 800 metres. This feature is well developed across the summit of Mont Rivel (807 metres). A fragment of the Champagnole surface is seen in the same hill, about 170 metres lower down.

The 'faisceau de Syam' (Fig. 9), the second structure that disturbs the continuity of the plateaux, is a north–south trending zone separating the Plateau de Champagnole from the Plateau de Levier-Nozeroy to the east. Structures of the faisceau or fold-bundle, may be seen south of Champagnole in the region of Billaude, Syam, and Sirod, with the gorges of the Lemme providing perhaps the best section of all. Most of these localities are on the N5, or within easy reach of it, and a short detour gives views of several well-exposed, small folds. As with the majority of structural features encountered so far, these structures were formed during the Alpine orogeny. The Euthe and the faisceau de Syam represent zones of weakness in the outer Jura. They, and others, were likely to have had some effect on the underlying basement, and during the Tertiary period they probably acted as buffer zones against the great forces developed during the Alpine movements. As many of the zones were graben structures, the strata within the downfaulted areas were compressed between the large blocks bearing the rocks of the Jurassic plateaux. The downfaulted rocks were consequently folded and further faulted; some, as we have witnessed in the Ledonian–Bisontin arc, were even overthrust.

Beyond Chaux-des-Crotenay to the south of Champagnole the plateaux of the external Jura finally give way to a second great landscape assemblage, that associated with various stages in the erosion of a system of parallel folds. (Fig. 10). As with the plateaux the formation of the fold system is linked with

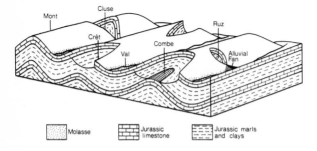

Fig. 10. This block diagram shows the variety of land-forms found in the folded Jura. Many of the local names used to describe these features have been applied elsewhere under similar geological conditions.

the building of the Alps. The folded strata are mainly Mesozoic in age and are essentially Jurassic. According to many experts the basement rocks remained essentially unaffected by the movement and the folded Jura are often regarded as the type example of epidermis folding. From the south-east of Chaux-des-Crotenay to Morez, the N5 follows an excellent, instructive route across the High Jura. The junction with the plateaux region is a thrust-plane, and an excellent road section near Fort-du-Plasne reveals that the thrust strata are of Upper Jurassic–Lower Cretaceous age. The main outcrop is in Kimmeridgian and Portlandian limestones which, once again, reveal the former extent of the carbonate-rich seas of the Jurassic period.

En route to Morez and beyond to La Cure the N5 crosses many anticlinal and synclinal structures. The scenic expression of these folds is not immediately apparent in the west, for they are bevelled by erosion surfaces, such as the high Nozeroy plateau south of Champagnole. However, when the N5 finally climbs to the Col de la Savine the relationship between structure and land-form becomes much closer. The Col is at the crest of one of the anticlines of the High Jura, that of Mont Noir. This is a fine example of 'normal' anticlinal relief, called a mont where the highest parts of structure and topography largely coincide. Even here, however, there is a complication. As the road descends from the Col to Morbier it passes over slightly younger rocks, suggesting that the crest of the anticline has been bevelled.

Further south-east the road passes across the corresponding syncline, whose axis to the south-west is followed by the valley of the River Bienne. This is a second example of normal relief, but in this case structural and topographic 'lows' coincide to form a 'val'. Landscapes are rarely as simple as this, however, and there is plenty of evidence in the vicinity of Morez to suggest a more complicated story. The syncline is cut by a transverse fault, exploited by erosion to form a valley occupied by the town (the Grande Rue is along the fault trace). The course of the Bienne, however, provides the main complication. Upstream of Morez it cuts through the Longchaumois syncline and the Arcets anticline. This discordant line is difficult to account for but some investigators have suggested that the stream came into existence before the episode of folding, and was able to maintain its course across the developing structures. Such streams are called antecedent, and they may be quite common in areas of recent earth movement.

So far we have seen examples of normal relief, but a more complicated stage in land-form development is displayed south-west of Les Rousses in the vicinity of Mont Fier. The remarkable feature of this hill is that structurally it corresponds to a syncline, and so provides one of the best examples in the Jura of inverted relief. It makes a fine contrast to the larger-scale inversion of the Bas-Boulonnais. The feature has developed because the adjacent anticlines are more readily eroded, leaving the intervening syncline as an upstanding feature. In the Mont Fier area the anticlines have been breached to form Combe Barthod to the north, and the Combe of Mont Fier to the south. The northern slope of Combe Barthod is a fine crêt whose scarp, together with the bulk of Mont Fier, dominates the view.

From Les Rousses to La Cure the route passes across the south-western end of the Vallée de Joux, which coincides with a major syncline. The floor of this valley is occupied by the Lac des Rousses, set in marshy surroundings that extend far to the north-east. This suggests very poor drainage, which is due to a combination of impermeable Cretaceous marls that line the valley floor and a veneer of debris laid down by a former glacier. In the area of La Cure, various sections, such as that between La Cure and La Faucille, reveal evidence for the presence of Lower Cretaceous rocks within the synclinal flexures of the region. Tertiary rocks were also affected by the folding and, within the High Jura, Tertiary sediments that rest unconformably on the Cretaceous have themselves been folded. This indicates that the last period of folding in the region was later than both the erosional surface and the deposition of these Tertiary rocks. Many of the folded Tertiary deposits of the High Jura are of Miocene age and the indications are that the fold phase is of late Miocene–Pliocene age.

The prevalence of rough pasture and woodland is perhaps the first impression that one gains of land use in the Jura. Lithology, terrain, and climate all restrict the scope of farming activity. Much of the region is carved in limestone, which as we have already seen, yields shallow, dry soils. In this instance, moreover, the problem of a thin soil cover is exacerbated by the widespread development of steep mountain slopes. And, as if this were not enough, the elevated nature of the High Jura makes for long, rather severe winters and heavy precipitation, both of which inhibit cultivation. Even on the Jura plateaux, therefore, conifer plantations are numerous and advertise the limited agricultural value of the land. They interrupt a landscape of rocky pastures devoted to cattle grazing, and which give way on steep ground to seminatural woods of oak, beech, and other broadleaved, deciduous hardwoods. Scattered pockets of meadow and plough land are, in fact, present on the plateaux. As might be expected, they indicate the development of deeper, moister soils. They are formed in a range of parent materials: moraines left by Alpine and local glaciers; Oxford Clay preserved in depressions in the limestone; and marls exposed by the removal of the limestone. Vineyards, too, have been planted on the more sheltered south-facing slopes, where quite reasonable amounts of sunshine are enjoyed during the summer.

An ascent of the folded Jura will soon make it obvious that the spruce woodlands clothing the mountainsides are different from the conifer plantations of the plateaux. The size and spacing of the trees are no longer uniform, for at these heights spruce grows naturally, being better adapted to the prevailing climatic rigours than the deciduous hardwoods. Increases in slope cause the trees to thin out and become stunted, as bare rock replaces soil; indeed, the limestone cliffs of the deeper valleys have little vegetation of any kind. The floors of the valley are commonly covered with Cretaceous clays and mixed debris from the erosion of the ridges above. The patchwork of cultivation seen on the valley floors is evidently made possible by these accumulations.

The descent of the hairpin bends of the Col de la Faucille reveals a magnificent view to the south over the Swiss Plateau and Lake Geneva, with the Alps providing a distant backcloth. On the smaller scale there are roadside cuttings in unconsolidated sands and gravels laid down by melting ice. Further signs of the work of former glaciers become particularly noticeable in the vicinity of Gex. This town stands on a gently sloping spread of debris deposited by meltwater that escaped during the decay of the ice. The debris mound has the form of a cone, which was centrally dissected by a final phase of meltwater activity. This fluvioglacial cone is itself developed on further glacial debris. Close inspection of the debris shows that much of it originated in the Jura, suggesting that this upland area generated its own glaciers. Locally, for example just north of Ornex, there are striking streamlined hummocks called drumlins. These are believed to have formed at the base of an actively advancing glacier. The fresh undulating appearance of this landscape suggests that it was formed quite recently, and investigators have proposed that the last glacial episode, called the Würm, was reponsible.

Looking out over the Swiss Plateau one can see a prosperous landscape of woodland, arable fields, and dairy pasture. The woodland, which mainly comprises fine stands of beech, is characteristically located on the steep limestone and sandstone slopes revealed in the valleys and depressions incised into the plateau. The irregular pattern and varied character of the farmland is not without significance either, for it reflects the heterogeneous composition of the drift deposits which mantle the plateau. As in the Jura, however, most of the vineyards are concentrated on sunny, south-facing slopes. Indeed, on the flights of terraces around the northern shores of Lake Geneva, they occur to the virtual exclusion of all other types of agriculture.

The Swiss Plateau to Genoa

The glacial deposits and land-forms south of Gex are part of a broad, poorly drained plateau that separates the High Jura from the Alps. This plateau is known geologically as the Molasse Basin, and the character of its constituent rocks can be determined from an examination of a few roadside cuttings. Sandstones and conglomerates are the dominant rock-types of the Molasse formation. They were deposited in the basin, or foredeep, during the uplift of the Jura and the Alps and, although most of the sediments were laid down under continental conditions, a few marine horizons have been recorded.

The Molasse deposits are relatively undisturbed although some minor folds and faults indicate that the Alpine movements continued until only a few million years ago. By comparison with the folded Jura the structures of the Molasse basin are insignificant, as indeed are those of the Jura when compared with their Alpine counterparts.

Beyond Geneva the Alpine mountain chain rises formidably above the Molasse basin and, as we shall discover, it forms the mountainous heart of Europe. The road from Geneva to Mont Blanc (Fig. 11) follows the valley of the River Arve as far as Chamonix. As one journeys south it soon becomes obvious that the valley has been extensively glaciated.

West of Bonneville the Arve flows through the relatively open basin of La Roche, which shows signs of both glacial erosion and deposition. The basin itself was overdeepened by an ancient glacier, and then partly filled with the debris laid down as the ice melted. Investigation has shown that the debris infill is complicated. There are two distinct moraines, crescent-shaped in plan; these are spreads of material directly dumped by the ice in the west of the basin. Local names may occasionally be helpful in indicating the character of such material; here, the upper deposit is called the moraine des Rocailles, an obvious reference to its blocky character. The centre of the basin is filled with a very fine-grained sediment, on which the village of Arenthon now rests. This material laid down in an Ice Age lake is being dissected by the Arve to form river terraces.

Alpine geology, especially for someone heading for the pleasures of the Mediterranean, is best viewed on the macroscopic scale, and the steep walls of the Arve valley and the faces of the mountains beyond present an ideal scene. A few well-chosen viewpoints will demonstrate various features: some observers may even be encouraged to formulate their own theories as to the way in which the visible structures were formed.

The Arve, east of Geneva, flows between the Massif de Borne-Aravais to the south, and the Pré-alpes du Chablais to the north. The rocks of the latter are well exposed on the northern wall of the valley and it is therefore possible to reconstruct a section across a classic klippe – that is the erosional remnant of a large, thrusted horizontal fold structure, or nappe. To observe the full splendour of the Arve valley it is worth making a detour to the hamlet of Mont Saxonnex which nestles high on the north-facing hillside opposite Marignier. The hamlet is about half-way between Bonneville and Cluses (Fig. 11), and on a clear day it is possible to observe most of the structural features of the Pré-alpes du Chablais. Our sketch of the area shows both the major and minor structural elements. The general structural grain suggests the idea of a gigantic thrust movement towards the north-west. Inspection of the lower slopes reveals a pronounced break of slope above the hamlet of Ayse. This feature extends almost as far as Marignier and it makes the line of contact between a number of small nappes and the underlying molasse, which is *in situ*, or autochthonous. Marignier itself sits

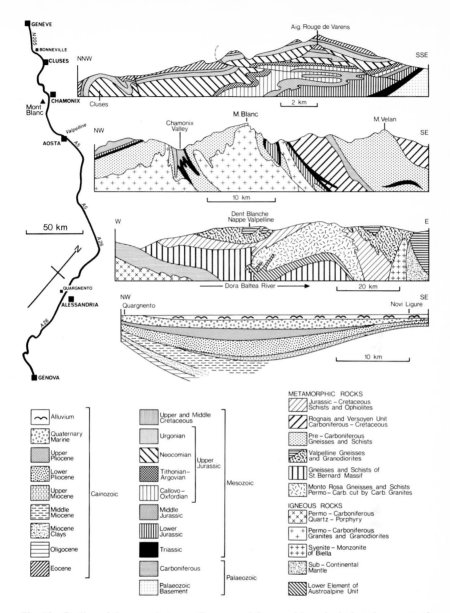

GENÈVE
N205
BONNEVILLE
CLUSES
CHAMONIX
Mont Blanc
AOSTA
Valpelline
A5
50 km
A26
QUARGNENTO
ALESSANDRIA
A26
GENOVA

NNW
Aig. Rouge de Varens
SSE
Cluses
2 km

NW
Chamonix Valley
M.Blanc
M.Velan
SE
10 km

W
Dent Blanche
Nappe Valpelline
E
Dora Baltea River
20 km

NW
Quargnento
SE
Novi Ligure
10 km

Alluvium

Quaternary Marine

Upper Pliocene

Lower Pliocene

Upper Miocene

Middle Miocene — Cainozoic

Miocene Clays

Oligocene

Eocene

Upper and Middle Cretaceous

Urgonian

Neocomian — Upper Jurassic

Tithonian–Argovian

Callovo–Oxfordian

Middle Jurassic

Lower Jurassic — Mesozoic

Triassic

Carboniferous

Palaeozoic Basement — Palaeozoic

METAMORPHIC ROCKS

Jurassic – Cretaceous Schists and Ophiolites

Rognais and Versoyen Unit Carboniferous – Cretaceous

Pre – Carboniferous Gneisses and Schists

Valpelline Gneisses and Granodiorites

Gneisses and Schists of St. Bernard Massif

Monto Rosa Gneisses and Schists Permo–Carb. cut by Carb. Granites

IGNEOUS ROCKS

Permo – Carboniferous Quartz – Porphyry

Permo – Carboniferous Granites and Granodiorites

Syenite – Monzonite of Biella

Sub – Continental Mantle

Lower Element of Austroalpine Unit

Fig. 11. Outline of the route between Geneva and Genoa with geological sections across the northern subalpine massif, the Mont Blanc massif, the Valpelline nappe and the Po Basin. These illustrate the complex nature of the Alps and the great thickness of sediment that filled the rapidly subsiding Po Basin during the Cainozoic.

35

on rocks of the Ultrahelvetic formation, and it is clear that these too have been thrust over the Molasse at Bonneville. In the near distance the skyline is dominated by the peaks of Le Môle and La Pointe d'Orchez; and beyond by the Pointe de Marcelly. The first two occur in the Median Pre-Alpine nappe; the second is the highest point of the Bréche nappe. Both nappes are composed of older Mesozoic rocks and once again they sit upon molasse and Ultrahelvetic sediments.

The valley of the Arve between Bonneville and Cluses is the site of much more recent events which can be seen from Mont Saxonnex (Fig. 13). The tributary streams of the Arve, attacking relatively weak Flysch sediments and glacial debris, have brought down great volumes of material which they have deposited to form a series of imposing fans (Fig. 12). One of the largest, deposited by the River Borne, is about 5 kilometres wide at its base and has pushed the Arve against the northern flank of the main valley. A further large fan, that of the braided River Giffre, has pushed the Arve to the south, where it is undercutting the valley wall. The village of Marignier stands towards the apex of the Giffre fan.

The fan sequence terminates at the town of Cluses, above which the Arve flows in an impressive gorge. The valley floor there narrows to little more than 300 metres, and is enclosed by high cliffs, down which tributary streams fall in cascades. It is not surprising that Cluses has given its name to this type of scenery, especially in the Jura, where similar examples can be seen. The origin of the gorge may be linked with the problem presented by the course of the Arve as a whole. The river was initiated on the surface of the north-west-plunging Morcles–Aravis nappe, in much the same way as water

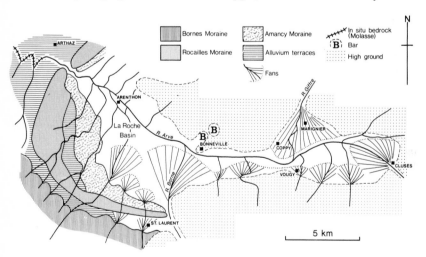

Fig. 12. The valley of the middle Arve. Note the series of fans laid down by active tributaries of the main river, and the crescentic moraine system in the west deposited by the former Arve glacier.

36

flows down the sloping roof of a house. Its detailed course has also been controlled by geological structure. Below Cluses the river flows in a syncline containing relatively soft sandstones and shales. Between Cluses and Sallanches its course is determined by a network of joints that form a weak zone in the limestone. The gorge of the Arve owes its character to tight nappe folding which multiplies the effect of a single resistant stratum.

The great limestone blocks of the forealps which flank the Arve Valley present a blend of forest, rough grassland, and restricted cultivation very reminiscent of that in the Jura. It seems reasonable to conclude that similar environmental and land-use agencies prevail. Forest is predictably most widely distributed on the steeper slopes, particularly those facing north and so experiencing the greatest shade. Within the forest a clear zonation of species is readily apparent. At an elevation of about 900 metres, beech, oak, and chestnut are succeeded by the much darker and evergreen spruce, silver fir, and, near the tree-line, Arolla pine as well. The tree-line reaches up to about 1600 metres on the shaded slopes, in contrast to the sunny slopes where it may exceed 2000 metres. Away from the valley sides, on the summits of the limestone blocks, much of the forest has been cleared, and large tracts of desolate, rocky terrain, almost bare of vegetation, are typical. The only arable farming in the area is on the valley floor, which for part of its length is excavated in soft Lower Jurassic shales. Orchards grow on the lower parts of the south-facing slopes, often with vineyards a little higher up. Neither is found on the valley floor itself, because of the risk of frost damage in spring, when cold, heavy air can pond in the bottom of the valley.

Along the Arve towards Cluses it is noticeable that the Ultrahelvetics rise

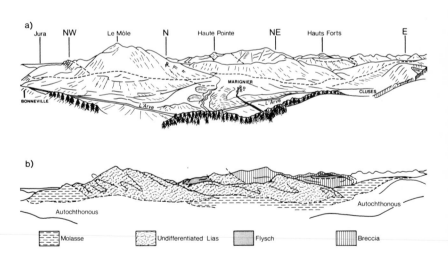

Fig. 13. (a) A view across the Arve valley from Mont Saxonnex towards Marignier.
(b) A section to show the basic geology as well as the relationship between allochthonous and autochthonous blocks of the above area.

up and over a well-defined anticline. To the south of this fold the Ultra-helvetics form the northern wall of the valley and mark the internal zone of the Pré-alpes du Chablais. Beyond this zone lie the Massif subalpin du Haut Griffe and the Massif Mont Blanc (Fig. 11). The former is a major unit of the Helvetic Alps, and the pronounced cliffs and sharp ridges of the region add to an already spectacular scenery. The rocks of the Haute Griffe are of Mesozoic–Tertiary age, and their general character is vastly different from that of the metamorphic and igneous rocks of the Massif Mont Blanc.

The upper section of the Arve, in the vicinity of Les Houches and Chamonix, is typical of Alpine scenery. The western wall of the Chamonix valley, which descends steeply from the fretted outline of the Aiguilles Rouges, shows most of the important landscape units. Between Planpraz and La Flégère one can examine elevated, amphitheatre-like hollows, or cirques, overhanging the high-angled valley wall, then steep recesses or couloirs, and finally a series of fine basal fans associated with torrents descending from the Aiguilles. The valley floor itself is irregular, being developed across a combination of bedrock, morainic material, and river debris.

The chief agent responsible for this scenery is glacial ice (Fig. 14) which once occupied the Chamonix valley and extended much further west. The Mer de Glace and Glacier d'Argentière are shrunken remnants of former tributaries to the Chamonix glacier. It overdeepened its valley and undercut the Aiguilles Rouges flank, leaving behind sheared triangular facets marking the positions of former valley-side spurs. Above the valley-side the cirques were fashioned by small lateral glaciers, but were left 'hanging' because the rate at which they were eroded was much less that that at which the main valley was being overdeepened.

As the main glaciers of the area advanced they pushed debris before them rather like bulldozers. When the ice melted its limits consequently became clearly visible in the form of terminal moraines. The local evidence suggests that two relatively recent advances may be identified. The first occurred about 11 000 years ago when the Argentière glacier advanced to a position just north of Le Lavancher where it laid down a fine terminal moraine. At the same time the Mer de Glace extended to Chamonix, so blocking the main valley and impounding a lake on whose site Le Lavancher now stands. The second more complex advance began in 1601 when the Mer de Glace pushed forward, destroying the hamlets of Châtelard and Bonanay between Les Tines and Les Bois. A less powerful surge occurred in 1825 and was recorded in contemporary sketches and writings. This time the glacier almost reached the upper houses of Les Bois, and some of them were damaged by boulders falling off the advancing ice front. The Côte du Piget moraine was laid down south of Le Lavancher, and this now provides a fine vantage point from which the Mer de Glace, the incised melt-water stream of the Arveyron, and the ice-scoured Rochers des Mottets can be inspected.

Fig. 14. View across the Chamonix valley from le Brevent. Note the almost flat, overdeepened floor of the main valley, the tumbled morainic ground in the middle distance which results from a former more extensive Mer de Glace, and the first shattered peaks of the Aiguille Verte and its neighbours with glaciers below.

Older moraines are less well dated and have often been worn down by later erosion, but scientists can at least determine the likely directions of glacial advance by a method whose principles you can check for yourself. The range of rock types in the Chamonix Basin is such that the source of a particular rock fragment found in a moraine may often be determined. For example, the moraine at Taconnaz is dominated by granitic debris and so was probably laid down by the Mer de Glace, originating on the flanks of Mont Blanc, and not by the more 'natural' Bossons glacier, which mainly carries schists.

There is visible evidence that other processes are now at work in the Chamonix valley. The high couloirs are occasionally swept by avalanches that transport vast quantities of debris in a single, catastrophic event. The south-east flank of the Aiguilles Rouges is scarred by gullies, cut by torrents so closely spaced that the intervening ridges are knife-edged, and so may be called arêtes. Between Chamonix and Les Houches a continuous series of fans has developed, deflecting the course of the Arve. The Cône de la Griaz has been the most active and has forced the Arve to raise its bed by several metres since the start of the nineteenth century. The evidence suggests that this river has been active over much of its length in the post-glacial period. It has incised the rock bar between Servoz and Les Houches by some 60 metres, and has cut a trench 80 metres deep into the Planet moraine. The transporting ability of the Arve is shown by examining the debris in its channel: at Argentière, blocks 30 to 40 centimetres in diameter are being transported during the active summer months.

In the High Alps it is immediately apparent that forest is more widespread than in the forealps, and is the most important vegetation zone. This is despite much felling of the lower parts for extra farmland and vineyards, and of the higher parts to increase the area of alpine pasture. The principal tree is now spruce, for the climate is drier and colder and so less tolerant of the other conifers with which it is associated in the forealps. A great deal of planting has taken place, as is evident from the relatively uniform character of many of the tree stands. Timber is still widely used for fuel, house building, and local industries, and this will be confirmed by even the most casual survey of the settlements. Apart from the resources they provide, the constant presence of plantations above many villages and hamlets also reminds us of the ever-present threat of avalanches in such mountainous country. The pastures above the forest continue upwards to the areas of scree and bare rock that surround the mountain peaks. They are grazed in the summer months by dairy cattle, taken up from the permanent valley villages. The small chalets dotted about the pastures are used only seasonally by the herdsmen. Perhaps an even more conspicuous feature of the slopes above the tree-line in summer, however, is the great variety of flowering plants which burst into colour during the short growing season. Many of the characteristic alpine flowers occur in the Mont Blanc Nature Park, but, they should not be picked.

Splendid panoramic views of the Mont Blanc massif and the surrounding region can be obtained from the highest téléferique stations of either the Chamonix or Courmayeur (Italy) districts. The massif is essentially a single structrual unit. The emplacement of the Mont Blanc granite and the subsequent metamorphism occurred during the Late Carboniferous. Mont Blanc itself is sited in the middle of the metamorphic contact zone, between the granite to the north-east and the ancient crystalline schists to the south-west. The zone is one of high-grade metamorphism and the mixed appearance of the granitic and schistose portions shows that migmatization has taken place. This entails the partial melting of the country rocks and the introduction of granitic fluids. The result is a coarse-grained gneissose rock, with bands of granite material dispersed rather irregularly within the metamorphic rocks rich in biotite and hornblende.

The tunnel that links the Arve valley with those of the Ferret and Dora Baltea cuts right through the Massif Mont Blanc. The journey through it is stimulating, but few motorists realize that the concrete tunnel linings hide not only a classic section but also the evidence for two of the great north-east to south-west-trending Alpine faults. These faults are linked with the uplift and exposure of the massif during the Cainozoic. Their orientation is at right-angles to the north-westerly direction of the main alpine push.

Contemporary glaciers are well developed in the country between Chamonix and Courmayeur, and many of them are readily accessible. One of the lowest glaciers in the Chamonix area is the Glacier des Bossons, which can be reached by a short walk along a marked trail from the access road to the Mont Blanc tunnel. The track finally reaches a steep ridge of rock debris, or lateral moraine, at the Chalet de Cerro beyond which the glacier itself can be examined. The edge of the ice stands some distance beyond the moraine, suggesting that the glacier has retreated after an earlier phase of deposition. A glance to the north shows that the ice has the same relationship to its end or terminal moraine.

A study of the glacier reveals much about its nature and activity. Bands of ice heavily loaded with rock debris can be seen along the ice margin, and these hint at the great eroding and transporting power of glaciers. Much clear ice is present, suggesting that melting and refreezing is a common process, and that rock debris may be incorporated in the ice by this mechanism. The surface of the glacier is highly irregular and fissured as a consequence of movement over an uneven floor. Rounded pot-holes, probably eroded by melt water, can be seen locally, and add to the chaotic nature of the surface. The Bossons glacier has shrunk some distance from its lateral and terminal moraine and this suggests a period of glacial retreat.

As on the Arve side, the southern flank of the Massif Mont Blanc (Plate 5) is banded by Jurassic sediments. These have been affected by low-grade metamorphism but a few fossils (belemnites and crinoids) still remain. The rocks occupy the hummocky ground around the village of Entrèves. Hand-specimens with chlorite and white micas are visible and the rocks exhibit a well-defined slaty cleavage. From Entrèves the road south follows the Dora Baltea valley through Courmayeur, Pautez, Arvier, and Aosta, (Fig. 11). The route also dissects the western region of the internal Penninic Zone (Pennides) which has frequently been referred to as the backbone of the Alps. The nappes of the Pennides are huge, essentially recumbent struc-tures, with a core of crystalline basement rocks enveloped by Triassic and Jurassic sediments. The nappes are arranged in a somewhat ill-defined sequence with the older Grand St Bernard and Monte Rosa nappes overlain by the Piémont nappe. The latter is in turn overlain by the nappes of the Austro–Alpine unit – the nappes of Dent Blanche and Monte Rosa.

The lowest rocks of this sequence crop out along the Dora Baltea between the hamlet of Le Champ and the village of Arvier. The rocks are essentially gneisses and they are part of the great Grand St Bernard Massif that extends north into Switzerland and south as far as Briançon. To the east of Arvier the gneisses are overlain by the mica-rich *schistes-lustres* of the Piémont nappe.

The outcrop of the *schistes* is apparent from the widening of the valley and the gentle, more rounded profile of the hill slopes. Originally these rocks were thinly bedded shales and sandstones and a few fossils remain to indicate that they are of Jurassic age. They occur in association with a suite of basic and ultrabasic rocks (ophiolites) which are thought to represent segments of the basaltic oceanic crust. The ophiolites crop out extensively to the south and east of Aosta and samples can easily be collected from several localities in the region of Châtillon. Alteration by hydrothermal activity has resulted in the conversion of the olivene and pyroxene to serpentine. In hand-specimen this change is reflected in the overall coloration, and the rocks have been aptly described as greenstones.

To the north of Aosta the scenery is dominated by the Massif of Mont Mary (2815 metres) and in the distance by the Dent Blanche massif (4257 metres). Together these form a major element of the alps in this region and their crystalline masses represent the relic cores of the huge Austro–alpine nappes that overlie the Piémont nappe. Further outcrops of Austro–alpine materials (Fig. 15) occur further south in the Sesia zone, which is cut by the Dora Baltea between Issogne and Ivrea. The crystalline rocks of this zone are very resistant and they form a formidable backcloth to the extensive lowlands of the Po Basin.

The descent of the Val d'Aosta reveals a further array of features that result from the action of glacial and post-glacial agents, and one can identify many of the processes and their results, particularly the dramatic forms of

Fig. 15. Strongly folded rocks in the Verrès region of the Dora Baltea Valley, Northern Italy.

glacial erosion (Plate 6). Some aspects of the scenery are worth particular note.

During the Würm the Val d'Aosta was occupied by a glacier which retreated as the climate became warmer. There were, however, quite long pauses when the ice front was stable and recessional moraines were formed. Evidence for these episodes may be studied near Courmayeur, Aosta, and Châtillon, where important 'still-stand' episodes occurred. When the ice finally melted, further processes left their imprint on the landscape. Major fans, similar to those of the Arve valley, were formed where mountain torrents met the Dora Baltea. A fine example may be studied at St Vincent, east of Châtillon, where the torrent Marmore deposited a fan which it subsequently dissected to form a striking gorge. There are similar fans at Fenis, midway between Châtillon and Aosta; at Verrès; and, largest of all, at Aosta. The Dora Baltea, deflected in several places by these fans, provides evidence that it is carrying much debris today. Its water has been described as 'peculiarly greyish-white, almost milk-coloured', especially in summer when glacial discharge is greatest. This colour is a result of high concentrations of sediment in suspension.

In the upper, east–west section of the Aosta valley, the vegetation retains a distinctly alpine character but is more varied than that to the north of Mont Blanc. The sombre stands of dark spruce are relieved by groups of larch. In summer the latter provide splashes of pale green hues, but larch, being a deciduous conifer, is correspondingly drab in winter. The conifers are in many places abruptly zoned according to species and age. These curious patterns result, in fact, from avalanche and landslide activity. Thus, recent avalanche sites and active screes are marked by a less complete tree cover, for the trees themselves tend to be uniformly young. The screes generally have an inverted fan-shape, which is usually picked out by the age differences between the trees. Further diversification occurs on the steepest slopes, for here grassland and bare rock dominate.

On descending the valley it is very noticeable that the small pastures of the valley bottom progressively give way to a more varied patchwork of cultivation which encroaches on to the lower hillsides. It is equally obvious that this transition is matched by a shift in the composition of the woodland covering the higher parts of the valley sides and in a steady increase in the height of the tree-line above the valley floor. In short the decrease in altitude and more southerly position have restricted the true alpine habitats to the mountain peaks that tower over the by-now much broader valley. The trees are mainly broadleaved hardwoods, including much evergreen oak, which, together with the recurrence of vineyards and fields of maize and tobacco, serve to remind us that we are approaching the Mediterranean region proper.

The town of Ivréa lies both at the exit of the Val d'Aosta and at the beginning of an arc of hills, about 90 kilometres in length, that extends out into the Po Valley, (Fig. 16). The general arrangement is well seen from Masino, in the centre of the amphitheatre. Towards the north-east one can identify the mountains behind Biella, while in the middle distance a smooth rampart of hills, the Serre de Ivréa, sweeps away to the south. The Serre provides a fine view of the central plain, the lakes of Viverone and Caldia, and the western flank of hills.

Clues to the origin of this remarkable landscape are provided by a traverse from Ivréa towards Biella. The road passes over a series of concentric ridges, and the occasional exposure reveals the unsorted, angular nature of the material. This evidence supports the view that the arc of hills makes up a giant terminal moraine, laid down by the glacier occupying the Val d'Aosta. The glacier was of impressive size: it has been calculated that the ice in the amphitheatre must have been about 400 metres thick, with a volume of some 144 cubic kilometres.

Detailed investigations have revealed the complicated way in which this landscape developed. Some of the outer moraine towards Biella is quite

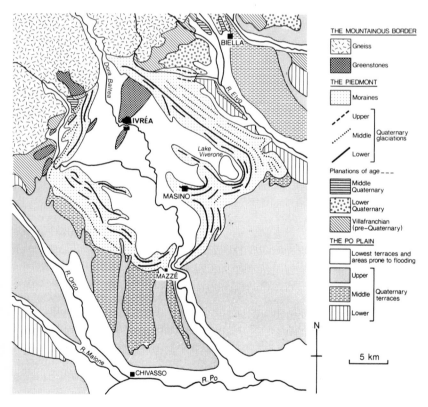

Fig. 16. The amphitheatre of Ivréa. Note the complicated way in which the surrounding morainic ramparts have been built up as a result of repeated glaciations.

deeply weathered and eroded by comparison with the fresher inner material, and this suggests that at least two separate glacial episodes have been involved. As the last glacier melted away part of the amphitheatre became a lake, of which a final surviving fragment can be seen near Viverone.

The road from Ivréa towards Vercelli finally leaves the morainic ridges at Cavaglia, and continues over a gently sloping cone of debris that was deposited by glacial meltwater. This gradually gives way to the flat plain of the Po (Fig. 11), which is mantled by recent sediments. This is a major agricultural area and few visitors will be unimpressed by the vast area devoted to the growing of rice. Structurally the basin is a region of strong crustal subsidence, a huge graben linked intimately with the post-orogenetic stage of the Alpine movement. Subsidence has been estimated at between 10 and 20 kilometres and it is therefore not difficult to understand why geologists have some difficulty in working out correlations between the Alps and Apennines.

Crossing the Po Basin, two contrasting vegetation patterns are seen. The first occurs as a relatively narrow outer zone round the north and south of the basin, adjoining the foothills of the Alps and northern Apennines respectively. Typically it comprises small areas of heathland dispersed amongst mixed farmland, where pasture predominates but where there is also a subordinate emphasis on such staples as maize, wheat, and the vine. Interestingly, lines of fruit trees have been planted in the fields; this is an ancient practice in several parts of Italy. The heathland hints at dry, sandy or stony soils. Inspection of the ploughed land will generally reveal somewhat finer-textured but similar soils. Evidently they are formed in the porous fluvio-glacial gravels which infill this peripheral belt of the basin.

In the central region, farther away from the mountains where the Po and its tributaries have their sources, the alluvial infill is much finer grained and hence more moisture retentive. Accentuating this tendency towards wetter soils, moreover, are the lines of springs which mark the boundary between the gravels and the alluvium. Naturally these are best developed in the north because the supply of water from the Alps is more reliable and plentiful. Water from the springs and even more from the rivers is used to irrigate the alluvial lands and the inner edge of the gravel zone. The water is carried from the rivers by canals, such as the Cavour canal, which enables 40 000 hectares to be irrigated between the Dora Baltea and Ticino rivers. Autostrada 10 crosses over this particular canal near Santhiá, to the north-west of Vercelli. A long, sunny, growing period in combination with the abundant irrigation water give rise to a more varied and productive agriculture than that of the drier gravelly deposits. Heavy crops of rice and up to seven cuttings of lucerne, clover, and hay are possible. The hay is used as fodder for dairy cattle, many of which are stall-fed. Other important crops are sugar beet, wheat, maize, and flax. Although the terrain is flat, elms, fruit trees, and, to a lesser extent, lombardy poplars line the fields and irrigation ditches. Together with the varied crop pattern they help create a diverse landscape which can give the false impression that it is one in which woodland is important.

Beyond the Po Basin, Cainozoic sediments crop out south-east of the beautiful medieval city of Casale Montferrato. To reach them one follows the road to Occimiano and Mirabello Montferrato, which climbs from the banks of the Po on to an extensive Holocene terrace. This terrace extends as far as Mirabello Montferrato, where it is succeeded by a higher terrace of Lower Pleistocene age. The height of this Lower Pleistocene terrace averages about 120 metres above sea-level, and a distinct break of slope separates it from the more resistant Cainozoic strata to the south. Around the hamlets of Mirabello Montferrato and Lu it is possible to examine sections of Eocene, Oligocene, Miocene, and Pliocene sediments, to collect fossils, and determine field relationships. The Eocene occurs as faulted blocks. The junctions between the Oliogocene, Miocene, and Pliocene are locally unconformable. Fossiliferous horizons are common in both Eocene and Miocene outcrops, with nummulites (foraminiferal protozoans) characterizing the former and bivalves and calcareous algae the latter.

The presence of unconformities suggests that significant erosional episodes have occurred, and these are locally exposed in the landscape as planation surfaces. An example occurs just north of Alessandria, where the high ground of Bric Rampuna is a planation surface trimming the crest of a structural dome. This surface now stands about 130 metres above the Po Plain. Many of the Montferrato surfaces were disturbed by post-Pliocene movements and then eroded, so that the highest ground tends to coincide with the most resistant rocks.

As Miocene and Pliocene sediments crop out just north of Alessandria, and are met with again at the mouth of the Scrivia valley to the south, it can be reasonably concluded that the structure of the Alessandria region is that of a downfold, or synform. The maximum thickness of Plio-Pleistocene sediments has been recorded between the Tanaro and Bormido rivers. The complete Miocene section between Serravalle and Rigoroso is renowned for its fossils, and careful collecting within the area will yield samples of many invertebrate phyla. Beyond Rigoroso the Miocene rests conformably on conglomerates and breccias of the Upper Oligocene. These in turn lie unconformably on marls of Upper Cretaceous age. The regional dip of the Cretaceous is to the south-east and, somewhat strangely, the River Scrivia follows the strike of the Montanesi marls and clays from Isolabuona to Genoa, a distance of approximately 25 kilometres.

Although the course of the Scrivia is partly controlled by geological conditions, it is similar to many other streams of the Ligurian Apennines in that it rises well to the south. This is rather surprising, for the Mediterranean streams are steeply graded and energetic, and might be expected to have extended themselves northwards at the expense of their more sluggish competitors flowing to the Po. The explanation for the actual situation is that the position of the present watershed, or dividing line between the two sets of streams, is a result of crustal movements, and the erosional work of streams has as yet had little impact.

As a finale to the geological section of our journey the rocks of the Montanesi formation are less spectacular than those of the Alps or Jura. They are, however, part of the Mont Antola unit of the northern Apennines, and to the sedimentologist this is a classic region in which to study the greywackes that were produced before the onset of the main phases of the Alpine Orogeny.

The journey

Our journey began in the relatively gentle landscapes developed on the blanket of weakly folded sediments that mantle the stable platforms of western Europe, reached a climax in the dramatic scenery of the Alpine orogenic belt, and has now ended in the more modest country of the Ligurian Apennines. We have examined many applications of sedimentological, palaeontological, and structural principles, and have seen how geologists can reconstruct past environments. The various agents that act on rocks and their structures to form scenery have been illustrated, and the importance of past processes in fashioning present relief should now be appreciated. The ways in which rocks and hill-slopes affect plant assemblages have been described, and we can now appreciate the great significance of Man in modifying these relationships.

The regional studies that follow apply these principles to a number of landscapes that, as well as being popular holiday areas, have a pronounced individuality, resulting from a close relationship between geology, scenery, and vegetation.

2 Snowdonia

Snowdonia is an area of outstanding interest to the naturalist, and also attracts large numbers of walkers and climbers to its wild and varied landscape. The rocks, land-forms, and vegetation of Snowdonia each make their own distinctive contribution to the scenery, but a knowledge of all three is necessary for the whole to be understood.

The geological history of Snowdonia spans 600 million years or more. Various rock types provide evidence of marine episodes and periods of explosive volcanic activity that once characterized the area. Around Snowdonia itself the rocks are folded into a broad, corrugated, saucer-shaped structure, called a synclinorium (Fig. 17). The axis of this structure has a north-east–south-west trend, the half-circle position occurring beyond Moel Hebog.

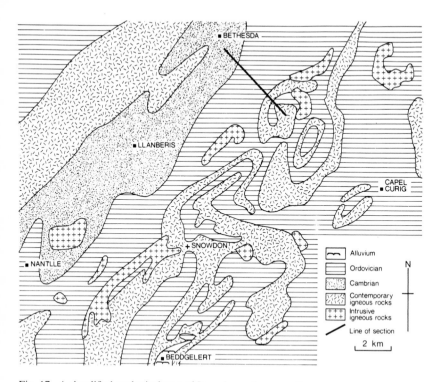

Fig. 17. A simplified geological map of Snowdon and surrounding areas.

A traverse south-east from Bethesda towards Cwm Idwal will reveal a fine array of geological features. The rocks visible in the valley-sides of Nant Ffrancon (Fig. 18) are of Cambro-Ordovician age, and represent over 100 million years of sediment deposition. Quarries in the Lower Cambrian slates at Bethesda (Figs. 19 and 20) and Llanberis reveal that the grain of the rocks trends across the valleys in a north-east–south-west direction, while the dip of the slates and succeeding strata is towards the south-west and the centre of the great synclinorium. The corrugations within the larger structure are clearly displayed in the sides of the major valleys. To stand and trace the symmetry of the downfolds of Cwm Idwal and Clogwen Du'r Arddu, or the strong upfolds of Tryfan and Gallt yr Ogof, is to appreciate the awesome compressional forces which formerly affected the area. Various pathways cross the mountains, with those from Llanberis to Pen-y-Pass and from Bethesda to Llyn Idwal perhaps offering the best opportunities for a study of the geology, and an appreciation of the influence of rock types and geological structures on relief.

The fine-grained nature of the slates in the quarries at Bethesda and Llanberis suggest deposition under quiet, deep-sea conditions. Intercalations of coarser-grained lenses, however, indicate energy fluctuations, when the action of the prevailing currents was strong enough to transport larger particles. The rare remains of the outer skeleton of the trilobite *Pseudatops viola* in the Upper Green Slate horizon dates the rocks at about 500 million years old (Lower Cambrian). The main body of slate passes downwards into coarse-grained, conglomeratic sediments and early Cambrian or Precambrian volcanic rocks known as the Arvonian Rhyolites. These can be studied in road-side exposures between Pentir and Llanddeiniolen on the B4366.

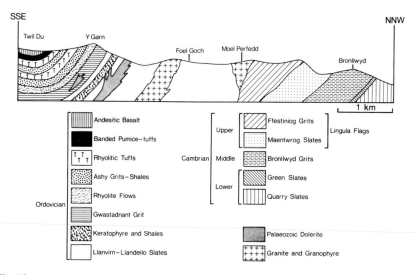

Fig. 18 A geological section along the ridge to the west of Nant Ffrancon, North Wales.

49

Snowdonia

Fig. 19. The Penrhyn slate quarries near Bethesda in North Wales. The Cambrian slates have been quarried for over 200 years and each of the galleries measures 20 metres in depth. Resistant igneous rocks cut across the slates as dykes, and the remnants of one of these can be seen in the floor of the quarry.

Coarser-grained sediments, the Bronllwyd Grits, also occur stratigraphically above the slates, and form the rounded summit of the Bronllwyd, north of Bethesda. These grits are massively bedded and very resistant to erosion. In Nant Ffrancon the differential resistance of the contrasting rock types is plainly evident, and in Cwm Ceunant the grits form the north-western cliff wall, the floor having been fashioned in the succeeding Maentwrog Slates. These weather to a rusty red, and their outcrop coincides with the low-lying tract between the older Bronllwyd Grits and the younger Ffestiniog Grits.

Once again the coarseness of the Ffestiniog Grits denotes a relatively high-energy depositional environment, and the presence of fossil ripple-marks (Plate 8) and the sinuous tracks of trilobites on the rock surfaces testify to a shallow, off-shore situation. The Ffestiniog Grits form the conical peak of Carnedd-y-Filiast which, like Bronllwyd, overlooks Nant Ffrancon. The grits are steeply inclined and display well-defined bedding planes: indeed, a single bedding plane coincides with much of the north wall of Cwm

50

Fig. 20. Workmen at the Penrhyn quarries use the slaty cleavage to split slates. In the past up to 6000 men worked in these quarries. Today, mechanization has reduced that number to 300.

Graianog. The southern wall of this particular cwm is formed by the compact crystalline rocks of the Moel Perfedd volcanic intrusion. These offered considerable resistance to the processes of glacial erosion which actually sculpted the cwm. The rocks of Moel Perfedd were probably forcefully intruded along the faulted junction between the Cambrian and Ordovician sediments. Other intrusions of similar lithological composition to the rocks of Moel Perfedd occur within the fold area of Snowdonia, but they probably relate to younger periods of Earth movement.

The fault that bounds the eastern margin of the Moel Perfedd intrusion follows a north-east–south-west trend. South of Llyn Peris, it marks the boundary between the Cambrian and lowest Ordovician rocks.

The Ordovician rocks of Snowdonia occupy the core of the great down-fold, with grits and slates of marine origin passing upwards without interruption into the Snowdon Volcanic Series. In the immediate vicinity of Snowdon, faulting affects the rock succession, and dykes and sills of crystalline rocks are common. In Nant Ffrancon the slates crop out between Moel Perfedd and the southern wall of Cywion, and are less resistant than the grits and igneous rocks. Thus, Cwms Perfedd and Bual, which occur entirely within the slate outcrop, are less impressive than the more southerly Cwm Gôch, whose high southern walls are composed of hard, crystalline rocks.

Above the Ordovician slates and grits the Snowdon Volcanic Series forms the rugged, precipitous peaks of central Snowdonia, with Snowdon, Y Lliwedd, Glyder Fawr, and Penyrole-wen standing high above the surrounding countryside. Nant Ffrancon, and in particular Cwm Idwal, again provides the best rock exposures, with the view from the northern end of Llyn Idwal, towards Glyder Fawr and Twll Du (the Devil's Kitchen), showing the succession within the Volcanic Series and the symmetry of the downfold. In fact, the very form of Cwm Idwal owes much to the rock types and structural planes within the Volcanic Series.

The development of scenery can be readily understood by focusing attention on a small portion of central Snowdonia, which provides a microcosm of the whole region. The road from Capel Curig towards Bangor offers a fine introduction to many of the characteristic land-forms. As the road gently climbs there is no hint of the dramatic landscape to come until the gradient eases and the imposing size of the valley suddenly becomes apparent. To the south stands the massive, craggy buttress of Gallt yr Ogof, while the bulk of the Carneddau is set back to the north. The small stream of the Llugwy appears dwarfed by the size of its valley as it finds its way through mounds and depressions. As the road flattens out the graceful, tilted form of Tryfan comes into view, cut diagonally by its heather terrace above which a network of rock climbs has been developed. The road passed the north-western slopes of Tryfan which are littered with boulders, some of the blocks being larger than a car. On the right is Llyn Ogwen, shallow in spite of its appearance (it is nowhere deeper than 3 metres) and beyond are the rugged slopes of Penyrole-wen. A small bouldery promontory juts out into the lake from the Tryfan side and, looking back along the road, one can see how it once continued unbroken as a tongue of debris extending down the north-west slope of Tryfan.

At the western end of Llyn Ogwen a rock-paved footpath climbs southwards to the amphitheatre of Cwm Idwal. This is one of the most famous land-forms in Britain. Its origin and shaping, and that of Snowdonia as a whole, puzzled scientists until the mid-nineteenth century when the fantastic explanations of the Victorians were replaced by the more sober arguments of the developing science of geology. From a vantage-point along the track, about half a kilometre south of Llyn Ogwen, one is surrounded by evidence for the development of the landscape.

The ground surface is littered with boulders rising out of a veneer of peat. Towards Cwm Idwal a low ridge hides Idwal lake (Plate 7). The higher areas to the right of the path show surfaces of bare rock, which appear smooth from a distance but which, on closer inspection, show important points of detail. The surfaces are shallowly grooved and cut, but not indiscriminately: it almost appears as though certain directions have preference. The scratchings and groovings are rarely smoothly continuous. They may stop abruptly, or peter out in a series of small pits, perhaps a centimetre in diameter. Occasionally crescentic grooves, running across the general trend, can be identified. Locally, large boulders are scattered randomly on the ground surface.

More evidence is supplied by a distant view. As the eye runs from the base of Tryfan, a fine crag is picked out. It is the northern edge of a steep ridge, Y Gribin, that descends from the Glyder range. The cliff face, a favoured rock-climbing site, shows bold buttresses and nearly vertical slabs. Against the foot of the cliff, slabs and blocks up to 10 metres in length lie scattered haphazardly.

A climb up a low ridge leads to a sudden view of Llyn Idwal (Fig. 21). From this point the form of the amphitheatre can be clearly seen, but before this evidence is discussed a further clue towards the understanding of the landscape has to be observed. Down the western side of the lake a series of steep-sided and smoothly undulating ridges (Fig. 22) stands out, running nearly parallel to the water's edge. Three-quarters of the way along the lake, and on the eastern side, another complex of hummocky mounds occurs, extending part way into the lake.

The form of the cwm itself is perhaps the best indication of its origin. Its precipitous backwall hangs threateningly over the lake. The side walls of the cwm are less steep, but the south-east flank stands at a sufficient angle (about 35°) for it to be one of the most famous rock-climbing localities in Snowdonia.

The various land-forms that we have noticed between Llyn Ogwen and Cwm Idwal were correctly identified by the 1840s as good evidence that

Fig. 21. A recent photograph of the Idwal Slabs and backwall. Note the rockfall on the right, a relic of frost action at the close of the Pleistocene.

53

mountain glaciers had once occupied Snowdonia. These land-forms were seen as being strikingly similar to those found just outside the present ice limits in Switzerland, which have been discussed in the Alpine Section of Chapter 1.

By the 1860s the similarity of Snowdonian and Swiss landscapes had led to a general acceptance of the idea of Welsh glaciers. The features that have been described are repeated again and again through Snowdonia. Cwm Idwal then, should be seen as the site of a large Ice Age glacier. Its backwall was the site of intense frost shattering as seasonal meltwater dripped from snow cornices at the top of the cliff, soaked into the rocks, and shattered them with the expansionary force of freezing. The glacier, fed by frequent snowfall on its surface, extended northward away from the cwm. The nature of its movement was probably complex. The study of present-day glaciers in similar positions suggests that it may have moved as though rotating along the arc of a circle of very large radius. The result may have been to

Fig. 22. Hummocky glacial moraine on the western shore of Llyn Idwal, which is in the middle distance. Penyrole-wen is in the background.

overdeepen its floor by abrasion, brought about by the ice grinding contained rock fragments against its bed. The grooved and scratched rock surfaces seen on the way to the cwm point to the reality of this process, and the lake itself may occupy a depression carved by the ice.

The amount of erosion (Fig. 23) done by the Idwal glacier, and by the other glaciers of Snowdonia, has intrigued scientists. It is a difficult question to decide because it is very hard to reconstruct the form of the area before it was occupied by ice. Locally, however, it is clear that a very great amount of erosion was carried out. The simplest piece of evidence is the form of the abrupt end of the Gribin ridge. It is easy to envisage a glacier, flowing from Idwal eastwards, shearing off the once more-extensive ridge, and to see that the amount of vertical erosion achieved is about equal to the present height of the Gribin cliff.

On a larger scale many of the more spectacular valleys of Snowdonia (Fig. 24) owe their form to the scouring action of major glaciers. The most dramatic example is provided by the Nant Ffrancon which may be examined from a vantage point a little to the west of the path from Ogwen to Idwal. This glacial trough was scoured and deepened by one of a number of ice streams that advanced across Snowdonia from the Merioneth Ice Cap which lay to the east. The ice cut through the former watershed between Penyr Ole-Wen and the Glyder range. An indication of the work achieved is

Fig. 23. Roche moutonnée, Nant Ffrancon, Snowdonia. This land-form is developed on a dyke which is flanked by soft Ordovician sediments. Note the polished surface, resulting from glacial abrasion.

provided by the height difference of 600 metres between the head of the Nant Ffrancon trough and the adjacent summits. Further evidence is provided by the height of the trough floor which is some 100 metres below the rock bar at its head.

Glaciers were effective in scouring and overdeepening the existing landscape (Fig. 25) but when they melted they dumped great volumes of the rock debris they had been carrying. The low ridge at the entrance to Cwm Idwal which sweeps from the sheared end of Y Gribin towards the Nant Ffrancon is the result of the dumping of sand, gravel, and rocks as the Idwal glacier melted away. It has been shown that the climate then warmed sufficiently for Snowdonia to be partly clothed with woodland and shrubs. However, about 8800 BC the climate cooled sufficiently for small glaciers to occupy sheltered north- and north-east-facing sites in Snowdonia. Among these was Cwm Idwal. When the last small Idwal glacier melted, its load of rock debris gave rise to the fresh mounds already described. This freshness is a reflection of their age: they were deposited about 8300 BC. These small, recent moraines are typical of many of the north-facing cwms of Snowdonia. For example Cwm Graianog, on the western side of the Nant Francon, has a pronounced crescentic terminal moraine which can clearly be seen from the road.

Fig. 24. Aerial view from Nantlle towards Snowdon. In the left foreground are quarries (1) opened up in Cambrian slates; beyond and to the centre is Llyn Nantlle Uchaf; (2) further beyond is the fine ice-scoured valley of Drws y Coed; (3) with the giant roche moutonnée of Clogwynygarreg (4) on its far side; Snowdon (5); and Cwmclogwyn (6) occupy the background. Ice accumulated in Cwmclogwyn and the Cwellyn Valley (see Fig. 25) and finally overflowed towards the site of Nantlle, cutting the trough of Drws y Coed through a once continuous ridge.

During this late glacial period, with small glaciers dotted about Snowdonia, the climate must have been bitterly cold. During the brief summer some meltwater was released as modest amounts of snow and ice thawed. Exposed mounds of rock debris were smoothed by meltwater, which carried away fine particles and left behind the coarser boulders. The outer moraine of Idwal, smoothed and boulder strewn, illustrates the result of this activity. However, a further process was at work, with much more dramatic results.

At the base of almost every cliff in Snowdonia is a steeply angled (normally 33°) spread of coarse debris. Much of this cliff-foot debris is the result of the shattering effect when water freezes in rock. A maximum theoretical tensile stress of 2100 kilograms per square centimetre can be generated. In practice it is much less, but still ample to shatter the most resistant rock, which yields at about 100 kilograms per square centimetre. During the Late Glacial, then, ice-sheared cliff faces were readily shattered by frost action and accumulated extensive screes.

That part of the Ice Age, when several glacial episodes affected Snowdonia, may have lasted 0.7 million years. A mere 10 000 years have passed since the last small cwm-glaciers melted. This is too short a time for the landscape-forming processes to have brought about significant change, yet there are

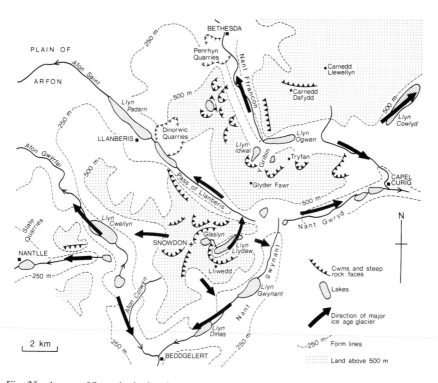

Fig. 25. A map of Snowdonia showing the directions in which the former glaciers moved.

many pointers to the work of erosion in post-glacial time. At Ogwen Falls the Afon Ogwen is cutting a deep gorge into ice-smoothed rock. Further down the valley, small landslides occasionally spread a thin scatter of broken rock across the main road. The late-glacial moraines in Cwm Idwal are slightly dissected by gullies descending from Y Garn.

And finally Man, particularly in the modern era, should be viewed as an erosional agent in his own right. The recently built track to Cwm Idwal is, during wet weather, the site of small-scale stream erosion, and a comparison of air photographs of the area taken at ten-year intervals reveals the amount of erosion resulting from heavy human use of the main pathways. The slopes of Snowdon itself are becoming quite badly eroded along the routes used by walkers, and many screes in Snowdonia are being re-mobilized by walkers running down them – those at Aber offer a good example. However, the imprint of the Ice Age is clearly dominant, and the land-forms of Snowdon should be viewed essentially as a relic of a past epoch.

A further integral part of the Snowdonian landscape is the mosaic of grassland, heath, and bog extending above the improved land of the hill farms. Yet until 3000 BC woodland prevailed to elevations of at least 500 metres, and though clearance began in prehistoric times, the present vegetation owes much to land-use changes in the modern historical period. Sheep-farming is now the dominant influence, but tourism, recreation, and field studies all have appreciable local significance.

Beyond the altitudinal limits of tree growth, on fertile crags and ledges inaccessible to grazing animals, exist scattered, remarkably diverse assemblages of plants, many of arctic and alpine affinity. The latter have survived from the late-glacial tundra of 10 000 years ago in refuges ecologically reminiscent of this earlier subarctic environment. Most of the summit vegetation is very monotonous, however, comprising patches of moss and sparse associations of grasses, sedges, and dwarf and heathy shrubs.

Below the summits, grassland is widespread, and bogs are common on the gentler hillsides and beside streams on gradual slopes. Heath is more restricted, to gradients between 30 and 40° that are well drained and often rocky, or developed on stabilized screes. While these plant communities typify upland Britain in general, in Snowdonia their importance in terms of area is significantly different. Bogs are not so widely distributed, for the highly dissected terrain promotes good drainage and thus inhibits peat growth. There is also less heath, due partly to a comparative abundance of basic rocks, which, on weathering, favour grasses rather than heathy plants; and partly because Welsh shepherds, unlike their Scottish counterparts, have tried to eliminate heather by burning, believing it to be a poor sheep fodder. The basic rocks, in so far as they have enhanced soil fertility, have additionally contributed to higher than average stocking densities for sheep, and grasses tend to replace heather and bilberry (another ubiquitous heathy shrub) as grazing intensity increases.

The main grassland species are sheep's fescue, common bent, mat grass, purple moor grass, and moor rush. The sweeter, more nutritious fescue and bent are subject to the heaviest grazing and yield fresh green turf wherever they dominate. The other two grasses and the moor rush are less palatable and, being deciduous, die back in winter, creating many fawn or almost white hillsides at that time of year. Bracken infestation is rife in the lower fescue–bent pastures and adds to the patchwork of colour by giving reddish-brown hues in the winter months. Of the heath plants, heather produces a dark mantle on hills and slopes and may appear virtually black in winter, whereas tracts of bilberry are greener and bushier, especially in spring. The bogs, too, can be picked out at a distance, either through the blackness of their peat where they are being actively eroded; or otherwise from the associated sheets of white cotton sedge, perhaps with some heather, or the dense swards of moor rush which are dark green in summer. The transitions between grassland, heath, and bog range from sharp to indistinct and, with the infinite internal variations, present an ever-changing array of pattern and colour.

These spatial variations are principally determined by burning and grazing, the precise effects depending on soil fertility and soil moisture. Traditionally in upland Britain, heather is burned in spring to destroy old, woody growth and stimulate young, succulent tissue. In Snowdonia, conversely, the aim has been to eradicate heather and increase grass coverage, so that heather is now greatly reduced and 'moor burning' not much in evidence. Heather is woody and burns more readily than bilberry or herbaceous plants, and grazing causes it to be stunted, with consequent loss of competitive vigour. In other words, burning or grazing, particularly if combined, discourages heather and favours plants less adversely affected. Bilberry is not so easily fired, and in any case can regenerate freely from underground storage organs, so that burning alone is unlikely to seriously reduce this species. It also suffers less from grazing, being avoided by sheep after spring. Hence, only where burning and grazing have a cumulative impact is it usual for bilberry to give way to grasses. If dry enough, grasslands with much mat grass, moor grass, and moor rush are also burned in early spring to remove dead foliage and allow sheep to get at the young shoots when they emerge. Bracken grows in most of the grassland on the lower, better-drained slopes, and here both burning and grazing help it to spread. Normally burning occurs when no living part of the plant is above ground, and even when the fronds do emerge they are unattractive to sheep.

Usually the greater part of the grassland is not easily set alight, so that grazing is really the key control on species composition. The coarse grasses and the moor rush are undergrazed after the first flush of spring growth, as they are then fibrous and tough. They thrive on badly-drained, peaty soils, and in such situations soon dominate if grazing is at all heavy. On drier slopes, the more palatable fescue and bent, along with varying admixtures of heather and bracken, manage to maintain themselves against the unwelcome pasture elements despite relentless grazing. At intermediate soil-moisture levels, however, within the tolerances of all the main grassland species, a mixed community develops, whose composition chiefly reflects grazing intensity.

Overall, it is clear that as the influence of burning and grazing increases the vegetation changes, in a predictable direction: heather → heather with bilberry → bilberry → bilberry with grasses → grasses → grasses with bracken → ending in extreme cases with bracken dominance on lower ground. In reality, of course, widely separated elements of this continuum can be found in close juxtaposition, either side of walls, fences, and any other feature which halts the advance of fire or affects the level of grazing pressure. The full range of vegetation types can be seen throughout Snowdonia, with typical examples on the sides of Nant Ffrancon and the adjacent mountains.

When these environmental relationships are set against a background of land-use history in Snowdonia, the transient nature of the vegetational landscape becomes apparent. Pollen from deep peats in the region shows that by about 500 BC, well into Iron Age times, heather moor had widely replaced forest. Possibly this early transformation related to a way of life, based on the seasonal movement of cattle and other animals, which came to characterize most of upland Wales in the Dark Ages and later Medieval period. In Snowdonia it actually persisted into the eighteenth century. During summer, stock was moved on to the mountain pastures, and cattle, being the least selective grazers of all farm animals, helped keep the undesirable pasture elements in check. Furthermore, treading by adult cattle limited the spread of bracken (as did the cutting of this plant for animal bedding, and the large-scale bracken burning which was practised until 1840 to supply potash and soda to the Lancashire soap industry). In addition to cattle, large herds of goats were kept to defoliate narrow ledges that might otherwise have proved a fatal attraction for cattle and, to a lesser extent, sheep. Goats fell out of favour in the eighteenth century, but impressive feral descendants of these animals still inhabit Tryfan.

The Great Enclosure Movement, which reached its climax between 1760 and 1830 in the uplands of North Wales, effectively ended the seasonal movement of stock. The hill grazings and wastes were enclosed as new farms independent of the older lowland units. Inadequate winter feed and shelter for cattle on these hill farms, together with the great extension of walled enclosure, made the change to sheep farming inevitable. The loss of cattle assisted in the spread of poor pasture species, especially bracken. Even so, many of the sheep which replaced the cattle were hardy wethers (male castrated sheep), left continuously on the mountain for up to five years. The wethers were necessarily forced to utilize even the coarse fodder elements, particularly when the latter were at their most vulnerable in spring. By the end of the First World War, demand for lamb had outstripped that for mature mutton, and consequently the proportion of wethers in the flocks declined dramatically. Again, this helped the expansion of plants of low nutritional value. Ewes and their lambs spend winter on low ground and are not returned to the mountain until April or May, by which time mat grass, moor grass, and moor rush are not very palatable. Inevitably, the brunt of the grazing is borne by the fescue–bent communities, leaving the inferior species to flourish.

It is evident, therefore that the vegetation of Snowdonia is far from natural. Few fragments of the original woodland cover remain, and the formerly extensive heathland derived from it has itself largely been replaced by acidic grassland, following a progressive intensification of land use. Over the last 200 years vegetational change has been mainly concentrated within the acidic grassland, where bracken, drab-coloured grasses, and rushes have proliferated at the expense of the better pasture grasses. Apart from coniferous afforestation, the newer land uses are connected with tourism, recreation, and educational visits. They are highly localized in space and time, so that while large parts of Snowdonia remain underutilized with respect to these activities, others are deteriorating from overuse. Undoubtedly there is a need to reconcile conflicts, where they genuinely arise, between agricultural, ecological, and recreational interests. Such an approach is vital, for if, say, agriculture were wholly subordinated to tourism, the existing vegetation and its landscape value would alter fundamentally. One way forward is the spatial zoning of incompatible activities, to conserve the region's resources and spread the tourist impact more evenly.

Snowdonia offers a fine illustration of two themes: the varying time-scales within which landscapes should be considered, and the importance of the interaction of the various components. The time factor is striking. Rocks over 600 million years old have been eroded by ice on a number of occasions during the past two million years, and a mere 5000 years of human activity have brought about profound changes in the vegetational mosaic. The theme of interaction, while locally important, may occasionally have little significance. Thus, rock structure has exercised a detailed and intricate control on the work of erosive agents, and yet the major valleys cut indiscriminately across the regional grain of the rocks. Similarly, the basic rocks offer nutrient-rich habitats for plant life, whereas the arrival of man has largely obscured the delicate relationship between lithology and vegetation. Snowdonia, then, is dominated by varying time perspectives, and by a complex interaction of elements in its landscape.

3 The Hampshire Basin

The Hampshire and London Basins are the two major regions of the British Isles essentially characterized by the presence of sediments deposited during the Tertiary Period. (Fig. 26). The Hampshire Basin is the smaller of the two with the Chalk of the Dorset Downs, Salisbury Plain, and South Downs marking its inland boundaries. In both cases the term 'basin' refers to the shallow structural forms of the regions. This is also true of the Belgian and Paris Basins, the four structures representing the distant ripples of the Alpine fold movement in northern Europe. The sediments preserved within the basins provide evidence of the geological history of the North Sea and surrounding areas during the last seventy million years. Movements of the Earth's crust in northern Europe during the Tertiary, that is between sixty-five and fifteen million years ago, are reflected in a repetition of sediments as large-scale cycles. Individual cycles imply an invasion by the sea, a gradual deepening, and then a reversal towards shallow marine and even terrestrial conditions. Mostly the sediments of the basins are soft and poorly cemented with sands and clays as the most common lithologies. Within these sediments fossil animals and plants occur frequently; they provide essential data for the reconstruction of past environments and climates.

During the Tertiary period the basins were linked within a single palaeo-geographic province; a shelf sea covering much of Denmark, northern Germany, The Low Countries, and south-east England. In Denmark, Belgium, and along the Essex coast evidence in the form of volcanic debris indicates the presence of once-active volcanoes in the Skagerrak area of the province. Volcanoes were also a feature of the terrestrial environments of Northern Ireland and north-west Scotland at this time, but no evidence for the transport of volcanic debris into the Hampshire Basin has yet been discovered. In itself this may be of limited significance but, knowing that the main advances of the sea had a south-westerly bias, it says much about the distribution of sedimentary particles.

Marine formations dominated the sedimentation that took place in south-east England during the Tertiary. River, estuarine, and deltaic deposits do occur however and, where present, reflect the influx of sediments from large rivers to the west and north-west. Approximately sixty million years ago such sediments were deposited off the eastern shoreline of a land mass upstanding in the area of the Midlands and south-west England. These deposits included the Reading Beds, which take their name from the town around which they are particularly well developed. Not surprisingly the choice of names for the various Tertiary formations is biased towards the locality where they were first described or where they reach their maximum development. Contemporary with, but to the east of, the Reading Beds were the Woolwich Beds, the clays and sands of which provide us with evidence of estuarine mud flats and shallow marine conditions.

Above the Woolwich and Reading Beds stratigraphically are the deposits of the London Clay. In the Hampshire Basin these were laid down at depths of approximately 10 to 50 metres, whereas in the east, Sheppey for example, the stiff blue clays of the formation were supposedly deposited in waters more than 100 metres in depth. Sandier sediments and a greater variety of fossils of organisms living on the sea floor at that period indicate a shallower depositional environment in the Hampshire Basin. Environmental reconstructions based on the animals and plants found in the London Clay indicate that warm-water organisms appeared earlier in the Hampshire Basin than elsewhere in south-east England. More than 500 species of plants, including palms and mangroves, have been discovered from various horizons in the London Clay and several indicate that tropical rain forests like those of modern-day Malaysia fringed the ancient shoreline.

Within the Hampshire Basin the thickness of the London Clay decreases westward from 91 metres in the eastern region of the Isle of Wight (Whitecliffe Bay) to less than 27 metres in Purbeck. This thinning is a reflection of the

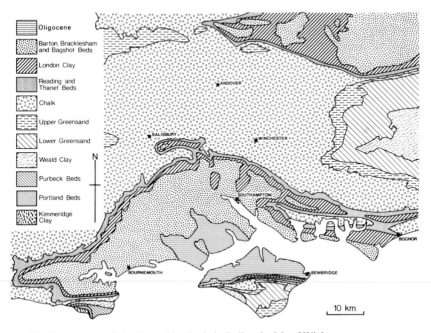

Fig. 26. The geology of the Hampshire Basin including the Isle of Wight.

advance of the London Clay sea from the east, for while the formation attains a thickness of 183 metres in Essex it is only a few metres thick in Wiltshire. Near Cranbourne in Dorset the formation is also known to overstep older Tertiary strata to rest unconformably on the Chalk. In the south-east of England the land formed by the cropping out of the London Clay is notably wet and heavy and in the recent past was extensively covered by oak forests.

These lands contrast greatly with those formed by the Bagshot Beds, the quartz-rich sands of which give rise to barren heathland. Once again local variations in sediment type do occur with the deltaic pipe-clays and leaf beds of the Bournemouth area passing laterally eastwards into marine deposits. On the Dorset Downs and Haldon Hills to the west gravels, assumed to be of Bagshot age, indicate an extensive denudation of upland regions. As in the London Clay period the presence of plant remains, including those of *Eucalyptus*, *Acacia*, and the monkey-puzzle tree *Araucaria* in clay lenses, indicate a continuation of tropical to sub-tropical conditions during the deposition of the Bagshots.

The picture of shallow-water conditions to the west and of offshore conditions to the east persists into the succeeding Bracklesham Formation. Around Bournemouth this formation is represented at first by the distal deposits of a river delta and then by sands, with pebble beds and thin coal seams typical of shallow coastal deposition. On the Isle of Wight the Alum Bay Sands (Fig. 27) represent estuarine conditions, with thin coal seams and black pebble horizons present within 178 metres of brightly coloured sands. Not surprisingly these sands are well known to most visitors to the island; the filling of tubes and various shaped bottles to create ingenious patterns providing entertainment for tourists of all ages. At the top of the sands fossiliferous sandy clays and clays occur which are often rich in the skeletons of microscopic organisms and molluscs. Some of these animals indicate that the area was once linked via open 'seaways' with the southern ocean called Tethys, the western part of which is now represented by the Mediterranean. The vertical attitude of the Bracklesham Beds at Alum Bay is convincing evidence of the effects of the Alpine Fold Movement; particularly when one compares their vertical stance with that of the strata of the type locality. In Bracklesham Bay the dip of the beds is almost negligible. Sandy clays indicate that in this area deposition took place in deeper water, with an abundance of oysters, other molluscs, and numerous vertebrates including turtles, crocodiles, and sharks as evidence of warm subtropical conditions.

The development in the Hampshire Basin of the Bracklesham Beds and overlying Tertiary strata is not repeated in the London Basin although sands of Bartonian age are known in the area of Windsor. These sands contain very few fossils, but sufficient evidence exists to allow correlation with the marine sands and clays of the type locality in Christchurch Bay on the Hampshire coast. At Barton the lower clay horizons often slump over the foreshore and

Fig. 27. Alum Bay on the Isle of Wight. Waters of the English Channel have cut deep into the soft Tertiary sands and clays, and the more resistant Chalk terminates in the Needles (to right of view). The view from the west shows the main outcrop of the Bracklesham Beds – the coloured sands of Alum Bay – as well as the London Clay and Reading Beds. The latter rest unconformably on the Chalk.

numerous mollusc and vertebrate fossils can be collected quite easily. At various levels within these beds fossils allied to forms now living in the Pacific Ocean have been found, while the general succession shows a gradual change from marine to more brackish-water conditions.

This change indicates the withdrawal of the Bartonian sea and the close of the Eocene Period. In the Oligocene which followed, the deposition of rocks was essentially confined once more to the Hampshire Basin with sands, silts, marls, and freshwater limestones representing mainly continental conditions. Marine advances did occur but these were limited in number, time, and extent. The final advance of the sea is marked by the presence of the marine clays of the Hamstead Beds on the Isle of Wight, which also mark the end of Tertiary sedimentation in southern England.

Resting on Hamstead Beds one finds superficial deposits of Quaternary age. In many areas these rest unconformably on older strata which have been tilted, folded, and faulted. This relationship indicates that between the laying down of the last of the Oligocene rocks and the formation of the superficials several episodes of crustal movement, uplift, and erosion affected the region.

A journey from Salisbury in Wiltshire to the New Forest and then to Beaulieu passes from rolling downland country with its panoramic views,

The Hampshire Basin

through gentle landscapes dominated by woodland and open heathland. This contrast reflects the marked change in the character of the underlying rocks, the downlands near Salisbury representing part of the broad semi-circle of chalk, which runs south-west through Dorset, and south-east towards Chichester.

Within this chalk rim (Fig. 28) the scenery owes its development and present character to variations in the resistance of the Tertiary rocks and, perhaps more importantly, to work by rivers and the sea during the past two million years. As the coast at Beaulieu is approached, the importance of a third major factor becomes apparent. This is a significant rise in sea-level, which reached its present height about 6000 years ago.

While the Tertiary rocks are generally soft and easily eroded, some strata are more resistant than others, with the Bagshot Sands, for example, tending to withstand the action of rain and rivers more effectively than the underlying clays. The result is that the narrow strip of London Clay and Reading Beds which runs close to the chalk rim has been opened up to form a discontinuous vale, overlooked by a relatively steep slope, or scarp, which faces in a generally northerly direction. This marks the edge of the resistant Bagshot Sands. The vale is traceable along an arc running from east of Southampton, round to Wimborne Minster, and is well shown along the Winchester–Southampton road. The vale is between 30 and 60 metres below the higher ground on either side.

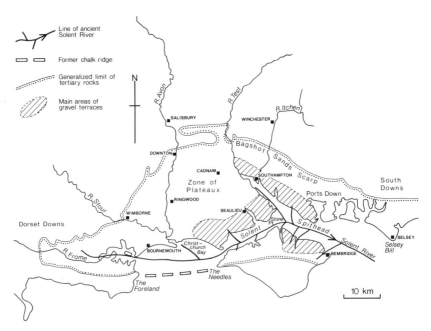

Fig. 28. Location map showing some of the main elements in the development of the scenery.

66

Of greater importance in the landscape, however, is a series of exposed, nearly flat surfaces or plateaux, which are being carved up by gullies and small streams so that they now have the appearance of flat-topped ridges. These are well displayed in the New Forest, and particularly in the triangular patch of country bounded by the roads between Downton, Cadnam, and Ringwood. The plateaux reach their highest point (127 metres) at Telegraph Hill, south-east of Downton, and then descend towards the south and south-west as a series of parallel ridges such as Deadman Hill, Hampton Ridge, Ibsley Common and Hasley Enclosure, Bushey Walk, and Hardy Cross.

A walk over the surface of any one of these ridges, at the junction where its flat top descends by a long slope to the adjacent stream, shows that it is mantled by a veneer of rock debris that contrasts strongly with the underlying Tertiary rocks. This surface debris consists largely of angular, brown-stained, chalk flints, together with small, white, quartz pebbles, fragments of sandstones and chert, and rounded pebbles probably derived from the underlying rocks. The now dissected patches of debris, sometimes referred to as Drift or Plateau Gravel, are believed to have formed more continuous sheets at an early stage in the development of the landscape, and have been used as evidence to illuminate events of the past two million years.

At the close of the Pliocene period sea-level was about 200 metres above its present level. This means that the area of the present Hampshire Basin was probably a large bay, with its ancient shoreline following the chalk rim. The following period, dominated by the Ice Ages, was characterized by major advances and retreats of the sea as the Earth's ice sheets alternately melted and reformed. The sea retreated from its maximum extent and, in so doing, exposed (as it does on a falling tide today) a wave-trimmed surface, bevelling the Tertiary rocks at a height of about 128 metres. This surface, covered by Plateau Gravel, has been described as the 'face of the block from which the scenery has been sculptured'. Fragments occur, as has been shown, in the north of the New Forest, and they may also be found on the Isle of Wight where rounded cobbles, indicating wave activity, occur on Brading Down at 125 metres. Further fragments may also be seen on Portsdown, north of Portsmouth, at 124 metres.

As time passed, various rises and falls of sea-level occurred but the dominant trend was for the shoreline to retreat. The newly exposed areas were occupied by extending streams, such as the Avon, Test, and Itchen, which followed the receding shoreline and occasionally cut sloping terraces by their own activities. Such terraces can be seen at about 91 metres above the Avon Valley. The gravels of the lowest terraces have yielded much information about early man. Flint implements of Palaeolithic type have been found in the valley of the Avon near Salisbury, and hand-axes have been recovered from the Stour Valley gravels around Bournemouth.

The gravel veneers tended to protect the underlying soft sands and clays from the agents of erosion, with the result that the northern edge of the Plateau Gravel country is marked by a discontinuous escarpment, running parallel to that resulting from the similarly resistant Bagshots.

It might be thought that the sea then steadily retreated to its present level, where it stayed, but this is not the case. Recent investigations have shown that the sequence of gravel-covered terraces extended as much as 46 metres below present sea-level. Offshore soundings have shown that at this time a major river, now drowned, continued the line of the Dorset Frome eastwards, through what is now Christchurch Bay, the Solent, and Spithead, and was joined by an important tributary, flowing down the site of Southampton Water. This reconstructed river is called the Solent River.

There is also good evidence that sea-level rose to, or just above, its present height before the last glacial advance of the Ice Age. At Stone, east of the Beaulieu River, and at Selsey, remains of marine organisms have been found which have been dated as some 100 000 years old. Supporting evidence may be seen on the Isle of Wight, where near Bembridge, ancient beach shingle may be seen resting on a platform cut at a height of some 7.6 metres above present sea-level. The shingle is mantled by a fine-grained, loamy material which was deposited by winds during the last cold episode of the Ice Age (Fig. 29).

Of more importance for the present landscape, however, was the melting of the last ice sheets. The sea-level rose, and the area between the Isle of Wight and the mainland was flooded. The southern rim of the Chalk downs, which had extended between the Isles of Wight and Purbeck was attacked and breached by the rising sea. The size of the gap between the Chalk cliffs of the Needles and the Foreland north of Swanage hints at the amount of erosion carried out. The low-lying country south-west of Bournemouth was flooded and now forms Poole Harbour. The Solent and Spithead became arms of the sea. Evidence derived from the dating of submerged peat below Southampton Water throws light on the later stages: the sea-level was 6 metres below the present during 7500 BC and 2 metres below about 3500 years BC.

The fine natural harbours and reaches of the Hampshire Basin owe their origin to this relatively recent rise in sea-level. Of particular note perhaps is the tidal estuary of the Beaulieu River where, at Bucklers Hard, Nelson's warship HMS *Agamemnon*, was built of New Forest oak.

For the past 6000 years or so the sea has been attacking the soft rocks that underlie much of the coastline (Fig. 30), with the result that quite rapid rates of coastal change have been recorded. The northern coast of the Isle of Wight, which is normally sheltered from the effects of high seas, has seen steady changes, especially in the clays of the Bembridge and Hamstead Beds. The average yearly rate of cliff-top retreat is about 35 to 60 centimetres. In Thorness Bay trees have been uprooted and carried seawards as a result of large-scale foundering (Fig. 31) while locally mud flows occur.

Fig. 29. Cold climate deposits derived from a chalk outcrop on the eastern side of Freshwater Bay, Isle of Wight. Their layered nature suggests changes in climatic conditions during deposition.

The mainland coast between Bournemouth and Hurst Castle has experienced rapid changes, although the impact is being lessened by sea defences. The western part of the shoreline between Southbourne and Hengistbury Head is protected by sea walls, but further east changes in the cliffs between Highcliffe and Milford-on-Sea are very rapid, increasing in intensity towards Barton, where the rate of retreat is about 61 centimetres per year. Further east towards Milford the rate of erosion is less, and further east still there is an important feature of accumulation, Hurst Castle spit, partly built of the material eroded from the west.

The central and western parts of the Hampshire Basin contain the most extensive tracts of open, seminatural vegetation in lowland Britain. Several contrasting habitats combine into a range of distinctive landscapes, some quite desolate, others of great aesthetic charm, and a number of them are of outstanding importance to our national wildlife heritage. They are, in fact, vestiges of an earlier rural economy, and have survived on Tertiary sands

Fig. 30. A rapidly eroding coastline, Compton Bay, Isle of Wight. Chalk occupies the immediate foreground, followed by Upper Greensand, the dark Gault Clay, and Wealden deposits.

Fig. 31. Recent landslip near Blackgang, Isle of Wight. Soft Mesozoic sediments are being actively undercut by the sea and weakened by percolating rainwater, with spectacular results.

and clays, or on the spreads of Pleistocene flint gravel. Under the primeval forest that once covered the entire region all three geological materials generally gave rise to soils of limited fertility. Successive phases of human exploitation spanning the subsequent 4000 years or so have left them severely impoverished and structurally degraded.

The diversity of vegetation that these soils now support is nevertheless striking, particularly in the New Forest. Here, a complex patchwork of unenclosed woodland (Fig. 32), heathland, grassland, and valley bog is interspersed with forestry enclosures of both conifers and hardwoods. Heaths and valley bogs that are an ecological continuation of those in the New Forest extend into Hampshire west of the River Avon and thence south-westward through east Dorset to the Isle of Purbeck. For descriptive convenience we shall refer to them collectively as the 'Dorset' heaths. Afforestation is no less apparent on these heaths, but hardwoods are generally absent and the dark blocks of conifers have a more monotonous aspect.

The spatial pattern and compositional character of the various plant communities have evolved since prehistoric times in response to traditional land use practices. Immediately after the Norman Conquest possibly as much as one-third of the kingdom was legally defined as Royal Forest. Although the areas concerned embraced much non-woodland, Forest Law suppressed cultivation and pastoralism to ensure adequate stocks of wild

Fig. 32. Ancient and ornamental woodland, Anses Wood, the New Forest. Behind the large oak on the right are several beeches, the one in the centre having been pollarded. Shrubs are sparse and there is little or no herbaceous vegetation.

animals for the hunt. In later centuries much of this land was deforested, especially on the better soils, as population growth stimulated agricultural expansion. Parallel with this development the emphasis within the remaining Royal Forests, including the New Forest, steadily shifted from deer conservation to timber production. On the unenclosed land of the New Forest and on the Dorset heaths commoners were allowed rights to graze their animals and collect fuel, as was the case on most other wastes and commons in southern England. Such rights still exist in places and, in a modernized form, are a central feature in the administration and management of the New Forest. The ancient legal status of the latter, incidentally, along with rights of common, help explain why so much uncultivated land persists in the Hampshire Basin. Innovations over the last 200 years have made its reclamation for more productive use a viable economic proposition. As it is, roughly two-thirds of the Dorset heaths which existed in 1811 have already been lost to forestry, agriculture, and urbanization, in part because common grazing assumed progressively less importance to the local population.

The New Forest is the largest Royal Forest, with a legal boundary, or perambulation, enclosing about 373 square kilometres. Roughly one-third of this area is privately owned, the remainder being Crown land. Enclosed and unenclosed woodland accounts for around only half of this Crown land today, and tends to be concentrated on the heavier, rather more fertile soils in the centre and south of the Forest. The present woods differ markedly from those which flourished prior to the arrival of the earliest prehistoric farmers. Pollen from peat in the Cranesmoor Bog south-west of Burley has revealed that, before about 3000 BC, oak, elm, lime, and alder were common, and that much hazel was present in the shrub layer below; birch and pine were very subordinate, and beech was scarce. Today oak remains plentiful, yet elm and lime have virtually gone. Holly has replaced hazel in the woodland understorey and also grows in conspicuous clumps known as hats or holmes that are scattered over the open forest. Birch, pine, and beech are all abundant.

In non-woodland habitats the contrast is even more profound, for heathland and grassland, which are so characteristic of the forest scene today, were simply not represented in the pollen record at the time in question. A comparison of pollen from soils below and on certain of the numerous Bronze Age (1800–500 BC) earthworks in the Forest, together with the abundance of the earthworks themselves, indicates that the first significant clearances and alteration of the original woodland cover were achieved by Bronze Age farmers. They combined cereal cultivation with pastoralism and these activities, possibly exacerbated by a deterioration of climate, effectively exhausted the soils, which were then progressively abandoned to the encroachment of heather and associated heath plants. Thereafter, until the Norman Conquest, the area seems to have remained largely uninhabited and given over to hunting.

The proportion that was actually wooded when William the Conqueror created the New Forest in the eleventh century is not certain. The Domesday Book shows, however, that afforestation was complete by 1086. Between the fifteenth and eighteenth centuries the interests of the Crown transferred from deer to forestry, as the demand for timber in the naval shipyards increased. The successful development of trees required the exclusion of deer and domestic stock, because browsing kills or injures seedlings and saplings. Initially, coppice banks surmounted by fences and circumscribed by ditches were periodically erected around 'mother' trees to promote natural regeneration. Derelict examples can still be seen in different parts of the New Forest. Eventually, more systematic afforestation became necessary, involving large-scale enclosure and deliberate planting and sowing. Three Acts were, therefore, passed to this end. The first, in 1698, led to roughly 1330 hectares of mixed oak and beech enclosures, in which sowings of hawthorn, blackthorn, holly, and yew were also made to protect the young tree crop from browsing animals. After the Act of 1808, 2700 hectares of oak plantations were established, and conifers were used for the first time, as windbreaks and nurses to the oaks. These plantations were heavily thinned to encourage the lateral branching that yielded the 'crooks' and 'knees' required by the shipyards. A further 4850 hectares were afforested following the Deer Removal Act of 1851. Apart from oak, much Scots pine was planted in its own right, together with lesser quantities of Corsican pine, Weymouth pine, Douglas fir, and Norway and Sitka spruces. Despite the depredations of the two world wars and normal rotational felling, original crops from these three stages of afforestation are present in many of the enclosures. Examples of the earliest enclosures, some retaining irregular outlines which coincide with older encoppicements, are Ocknell, South and North Bentley Inclosures, Priors Acre, Etherise, and Long Beech. A surprising number of the original trees still survive. On the other hand most of the early nineteenth-century plantations have long been cleared, but important exceptions are Amberwood, Island Thorns, and Backley Inclosures. Of the coniferous plantations, Milkham and Slufters Inclosures are among the largest. More recently, the 1949 Act allowed for up to 2000 hectares of additional planting, subject to the approval of the Verderers, or official representatives who safeguard the common rights. Consent for 800 hectares of new enclosures was forthcoming in 1958, and they have since been laid out. Some of the Verderers Inclosures provide a partial screen for the industrial development between Dibden and Fawley.

Thus, there are now almost 8000 hectares of statutory timber enclosures of which a maximum of nearly 7300 hectares may be fenced at any one time. The Forestry Commission, which was given overall responsibility for the management of the New Forest in 1923, has undertaken to maintain 50 per cent of the total woodland under hardwoods, so that the corresponding figure for the area inside the enclosures works out at just over 30 per cent.

The long and chequered history of the enclosures has endowed them with an exceptionally fine range of species and age classes. This diversity has been reinforced over several decades by management policies that have had a high regard for amenity. Even during the last war large clear-fellings were avoided by preserving belts or groups of timber. Similarly, from the 1920s onwards, the practice of leaving 'mother' trees for purposes of natural regeneration gained favour, and it is now the preferred method of restocking wherever possible. For the sake of amenity, 80 per cent of the edges of the enclosures have been left largely undisturbed for over fifty years.

Outside the enclosures are an estimated 18 000 hectares of commonable land. Approximately 3240 hectares are 'Ancient and Ornamental Woodlands'. Three generations of trees can be identified in these woodlands, although one or both of the younger, less distinct generations may be lacking at some sites. Beneath the trees there is typically an understorey of holly, growing in a sparse, essentially grassy, ground flora. Mature beeches and, to a lesser extent, oaks dominate the oldest generation, and many of them have in the past been pollarded, that is repeatedly cut 2–4 metres above the ground to provide winter fodder for deer, and wood for fuel. Interestingly, pollarding was outlawed in the 1698 Act because it inhibited the growth of large, structural timber, which by then was in short supply. Tree-ring investigations, on the other hand, have shown that the generation as a whole dates from 1650 to 1750, probably as a result of a concerted effort at afforestation in temporary encoppicements. The two younger generations arose within gaps in the canopy of the older one and around the woodland margins. Their composition is decidedly more variable for in addition to oak and beech, birch, ash, sycamore, chestnut, and Scots pine are quite common. Both generations have been attributed to reductions in grazing pressure, after the Deer Removal Act of 1851 and again after the decrease of stocking densities in the late 1930s and early 1940s. Grazing also has much to do with the paucity of ground flora, and with the prevalence of holly to the near exclusion of other shrubs like hazel. Good examples of the communities described here are Mark Ash Wood, Bratley Wood, Redshoot Wood, and Matley Wood.

Heather-dominated vegetation accounts for another 7300 hectares of un-enclosed land. It coincides with highly acid soils on the poorer sands and gravels which are notably extensive in the northern parts of the Forest. Usually the intensity of grazing alone is insufficient to prevent woodland spreading across the heaths; indeed, about 690 hectares of former heathland now carry self-sown Scots pine. Were the process to go unchecked the rough grazing available to the commoners would soon be dramatically diminished. For this reason the Forestry Commission is obliged to burn, and in places cut, about 800 hectares of heathland annually. The result is an uneven-aged mosaic of heather and heathy plants, ranging up to twelve years old.

Acidic grasslands amounting to 4450 hectares in all are distributed over the comparatively fertile plateaux in the south of the Forest. They are widely located on the sides of valleys and basins, where there is a beneficial flushing effect by mineral-enriched water draining off the intervening higher ground. Grazing is heavier on the grasslands and appears to be the main factor preventing woodland encroachment at present, but the occasional fires are no doubt important as well. Improved grazing is found on the 485 hectares of acidic grasslands that were reseeded and fertilized between 1941 and 1959; even so the best pasturage is situated on the Forest 'lawns'. These grow on stream banks – where there is a supply of minerals from the stream water – and in woodland glades on the better soils. Lawns are also a feature of many roadsides, for animals congregate here to obtain food from cars. No doubt animal droppings contribute significantly to the higher nutrient status of the lawn soils.

Finally with regard to the New Forest, valley bogs and communities transitional to them occupy around 2800 hectares especially in the lower-lying, more poorly drained southern areas. Those bogs receiving drainage water from the less sterile districts have an appreciable variety of plant life as well as the ubiquitous bog mosses and there is frequently a central strip of alder carr woodland. Conversely, where the drainage water is neutral or acid, the floristic variety is much smaller and alder carr is either absent or replaced by willow-birch carr. An accessible example of carr woodland occurs in Matley Bog, south-east of Lyndhurst.

We turn now to the 'Dorset' heaths. In 1811 these heaths covered about 30 000 hectares in large, continuous expanses of open land. By 1960 only 10 000 hectares remained, in over a hundred separate fragments, and the reduction and fragmentation continues to the present, for the reasons already given. As in the New Forest the *raison d'être* for the heathland was the common grazing it provided, so controlled burning was regularly employed to maintain relatively youthful stands of heather and prevent reversion to woodland. Nowadays there is little grazing and fires are mainly accidental. The larger blocks of heath are actually burned more extensively and frequently than in earlier years since they now attract more visitors. This has created a low, uniform growth of heather, quite unlike the compartments of different ages that were produced by rotational burning on a cycle of up to fifteen years. On the smaller remnants of heath grazing, if it occurs, is more intense, since these remnants are more isolated, and has the effect of encouraging acidic grasses at the expense of heather. In the absence of grazing pinewoods develop instead, the parent trees being in the near-by plantations, or their self-sown descendants on the open heath.

The gentle landscapes of the Hampshire Basin lack the drama of Snowdonia or the striking diversity of the south-west, but they offer instead subtle variations of character that owe much to a delicate interplay between rock type, erosional agents, and human activity. The rocks of the Hampshire

Basin are normally unresisting sediments whose varying character reflects changes in despositional environment between continental and marine conditions. The large quantities of fossils to be found in them have allowed detailed reconstructions of those ancient environments. During the last two million years, erosional agents have planed across these soft rocks with relative ease, and the resulting plateau surfaces have been shallowly dissected by present-day streams.

During the last four thousand years or so, human activity, combined with pervasive geological and geomorphological controls, has acted on the primeval woodland to bring about a range of plant communities that provide significant contrasts in the landscape. The original forest has been replaced by a patchwork of heathland on the poorer sands and gravels, bogs in the shallow valleys and depressions, grassland on valley sides, and woodlands on the more fertile soils. Throughout history the balance between these components of the patchwork has been determined by the varying ways in which man has managed his natural environment.

4 South-west England

The area referred to as south-west England lies to the south of a line drawn from Teignmouth in the east to Bude in the west. It covers, therefore, the whole of Cornwall and the southern part of Devon. Geologically, the region comprises, in the main, a vast tract of Devonian rocks into which are emplaced a number of associated granite masses (Fig. 33). Start Point and Bolt Head in southern Devon and the area just to the north of the Lizard in south-east Cornwall, are characterized by the presence of older, Lower Palaeozoic rocks, which have been thrust northwards over the Devonian. The rocks of south Devon and Cornwall form the southern limits of a great U-shaped fold, the centre of which lies to the north of Dartmoor and is occupied by the mixed, essentially marine sediments of the Carboniferous Culm. These last materials show a less striking association of landforms and vegetational communities than the regions of older Palaeozoic and granite rocks.

Throughout the south-west the scenery is intimately linked with the character and structure of the rocks. In the south the cliffs of Land's End are carved in granitic rocks with the regular joint patterns resulting in a castellated ruggedness. Elsewhere the granite outcrop is expressed as rugged tors (Plate 10) above poorly drained moorlands. Joints, faults, bedding, and cleavage are also important to the geomorphology of non-granitic areas, as with the high buttressed cliffs of the Devonian of the Tintagel region and the coves and headlands of the Lizard complex. Resistant rocks form promontories throughout the region with the examples of Hope's Nose and Berry Head occurring to the north and south of Tor Bay. Inland hard sandstones, limestones, and volcanic rocks form prominent ridges, while shale outcrops can be linked with vales and heathlands. The south-west was one of the first areas to be studied geologically and rocks of the area retain vital information on the early history of this region of Europe.

The major fold structure of the south-west was formed at the end of the Palaeozoic Era, within the Amorican arc of the great Variscan Earth Movement. The term Amorican stems from the Roman name for Brittany (Armorica), whereas Variscan was the name given by the geologist, Suess, to a fold movement, the centre of which was in south-west Europe.

The oldest rocks in the south-west of England crop out on the Lizard (Fig. 34), and it is probable that some of the altered or metamorphosed rocks of this complex region are 800 million years old. Much of their original sedimentary or volcanic character has been destroyed owing to pressure or heat

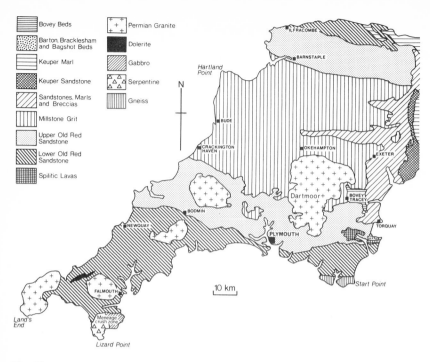

Bovey Beds

Barton, Bracklesham and Bagshot Beds

Keuper Marl

Keuper Sandstone

Sandstones, Marls and Breccias

Millstone Grit

Upper Old Red Sandstone

Lower Old Red Sandstone

Spilitic Lavas

Permian Granite

Dolerite

Gabbro

Serpentine

Gneiss

ILFRACOMBE

BARNSTAPLE

Hartland Point

N

BUDE

CRACKINGTON HAVEN

OKEHAMPTON

EXETER

Dartmoor

BOVEY TRACEY

BODMIN

PLYMOUTH

NEWQUAY

TORQUAY

10 km

Start Point

FALMOUTH

Land's End

Meneage crush zone

Lizard Point

Fig. 33. An outline map of the geology of south-west England.

Fig. 34. The weathering of the granite has taken place along well defined joint systems. Coastal view of the Lizard Point, Cornwall.

or both; the effects of thermal and regional metamorphism being reflected by the presence of the minerals andalusite, cordierite, staurolite, and kyanite. Igneous rocks of gabbroic, doleritic, and granitic textures are intruded into the older metamorphic and serpentine-rich rocks of the region.

Lenses of rock believed to be of Lower Palaeozoic age crop out to the north of the Lizard, in the Meneage crush zone. The lenses, often 1500 metres in length, are associated with Devonian conglomerates and breccias and it is thought that they occur fairly close to their original area of deposition. Fossils from various lenses indicate that the rocks are of Ordovician and Silurian age. In the Perhaver and Catasuent area fossil molluscs and brachiopods give a Silurian age to the Orthoceras limestone. It has been suggested that the presence of these Lower Palaeozoic rocks in association with Devonian strata and marine volcanic rocks, is an indication of submarine faulting at the boundary between an ancient land mass and a large linear basin, within which a considerable thickness of sediments had accumulated (geosyncline).

Much of the sedimentation that took place within the Amorican 'geosyncline' occurred during Devonian times, the sediments of south-west England provide many clues for the reconstruction of the environments that existed between 415 and 370 million years ago. The 'geosyncline' stretched east–west across central Germany, Belgium, northern France, and the south of England. To the north the shoreline of the 'Old Red Sandstone Continent' ran east–west to the south of Wales, through Kent, and on into Belgium and Germany. As with the Central French Island the Old Red Sandstone Continent exerted considerable geographical control over the deposition of sedimentary materials. Continental, near-shore, and deep-water sediments of Devonian age crop out in south-west England and the indication is that the passage from terrestrial into basinal conditions is from north to south.

Environmental conditions varied in given areas throughout the duration of the Devonian, however, and it is possible in areas of Tintagel and Newquay, central Cornwall, and central Devon to observe, in Lower Devonian rocks, the change from brackish-water to marine conditions. The lowest Devonian formation, the Dartmouth Slates, is exposed in the regions of Dartmouth (Start Bay), Newquay (Watergate Bay), Polperro, and the neighbouring, rugged and isolated Llantivet Bay. Dartmouth in the east and Newquay in the west mark the general westerly trend of the slate outcrop, the major components of which are purple or grey–green in colour, with a clay particle-size and a well-marked slaty cleavage. Interbedded sandstones, conglomerates, and volcanic rocks are common, however, and the sediments are an indication of a complex fresh- to brackish-water environment. The various rock types and depositional phenomena enable the sedimentologist to reconstruct a model characterized by rivers, lakes, and deltas.

The volcanic rocks within the Dartmouth Slates are essentially the result of ancient explosive episodes and occur mainly on the eastern part of the outcrop. Pyroclastic or volcanic air-fall deposits near Stoke Climsland in south Devon herald the start of a period of volcanic activity which was to last over forty million years. Ash falls may have covered large tracts of land and water, and possibly influenced the distribution of both plants and animals. In fact, the Dartmouth Slates have yielded little except for the fragmentary remains of several species of the emergent, jawless fishes. To the north, terrestrial rocks of slightly younger age have yielded evidence of a primitive sedge flora.

By Middle Devonian times the sea covered Cornwall and Devon, and the presence of different sediments once again reflects the palaeogeography of the times. According to some authorities, a mountain range with flanking river deltas was present to the north of a line from Ilfracombe in the west to the Quantock Hills in the north-east. A shallow sea with sandbanks flanked this range and covered much of north Devon. Hartland Point near Ilfracombe, and Silverton to the north of Exeter mark the southern extent of the shallows; a deeper sea characterized by the continuous deposition of sediments occurring to the south.

The area of the shallow sea to the north is characterized by marine shales and limestones such as the Ilfracombe Beds which have intercalations of deltaic sediments. Abundant fossil corals in the limestones indicate that the waters of this sea were warm, clear, and well oxygenated. Similar conditions must have existed around Torquay, Plymouth, and Chudleigh at this time, for thick, richly fossiliferous limestones indicate shallow regions within the deep-water realm. At Daddyhole, a short walk from Torquay Harbour, the limestones are dark grey and packed with beautifully preserved corals. At Walls Hill Quarry in Torquay, and Richmond Walk Quarry in Plymouth, however, the limestones are light grey in colour and more massive in their outcrop. The dominant fossils of these beds are stromatoporoids, distant relatives of the freshwater animal, *Hydra*. The quarries reflect the role of the limestones in local building with certain horizons such as the Petit Tor marble, from the Torquay region, having great value as decorative stones.

The reefs of the Middle Devonian developed on, or around, small islands formed on the sea floor by the accumulation of lavas and ashes. These reflect contemporaneous igneous activity, the maximum development of which occurred in the region of Totnes. Occasionally, the ashes and lavas are interbedded with fossiliferous limestones. The presence of two thin ash bands to the north of Torquay represent the distant air-fall component of this eruptive phase.

In south-west Cornwall outcrops of the Gramscatho and Mylor Beds with greywackes, grey slates, cherts, and spilitic lavas are indicative of deeper-water conditions in Middle Devonian times. The thick sequence of sediments deposited in an east–west trending trough, the floor of which was ruptured by Earth movements. Through the resulting fissures hot, spilitic lavas flowed on to the sea bed.

Fine-grained rocks succeeded the limestone sequence in south Devon and the grey slates of Cornwall in the Upper Devonian. The main outcrop of these sediments lies between the Dartmoor and Bodmin Moor granites, with coastal exposures to the east and west marking the true extent of the area originally covered by these rocks. At Pentire Head, near Padstow, 61 metres of pillow lavas represent a continuation of sub-marine volcanicity, whereas the sediments, altered to slates in Devon and to phyllites near Tintagel, are an indication of the extension of deeper-water environments. On rare occasions the Upper Devonian slates yield the fossils of goniatites, trilobites, and bivalves with similar fossils being more frequently found in the thin limestones of the Chudleigh district. Around Tintagel on the west coast of Cornwall, the Upper Devonian slates were once quarried for roofing materials and at Delabole the flattened, deformed shells of the brachiopod *Spirifer verneuili* were sold as 'Delabole butterflies'.

Coarse sediments between Gorran Haven and Mullian Cove are evidence of the palaeogeographic controls exercised in the southern Cornish area by the Brittany land mass. The sediments known as the Veryan Series have been dated, on fossil evidence, as Upper Devonian. To the north, similar controls on sedimentation were responsible for the presence of the non-marine Old Red Sandstone deposits in north Devon. At the end of the Devonian the sea migrated northwards over these deposits to reach its most northerly position and continuous sedimentation took place through Carboniferous times.

In south-west England the southern boundary of the main Carboniferous outcrop occurs to the south of Boscastle. It extends westwards from the coast to Launceston and then encircles the northern half of Dartmoor. No exposure is present on the west coast. The Carboniferous rocks are collectively termed the Culm Measures, the word culm having a possible link with the old English and Gallic words for coal or knot. The depositional environments of the Culm covered a region similar to that of the Devonian, the depositional trough having an east–west trend. As with Devonian rocks, those of the Carboniferous are often altered and deformed, with the exposures in the south being faulted and thrust to give a discontinuous outcrop.

At Boscastle the fine-grained sediments of the Lower Culm have been metamorphosed to phyllites. However, fossils, including trilobites, have been discovered and these may indicate a link with the more fossiliferous, slightly older Yeolmbridge Beds. It is likely that the two formations form a transitional series across the Devonian–Carboniferous boundary. To the south-west of Boscastle younger formations contain thin limestones and sandstones while a variety of volcanic rocks, cropping out in cliffs, mark the continuation of eruptive volcanicity. Resistant cherts are a feature of the upper horizons of the Lower Culm, excellent exposures occurring at Fire Beacon Point and Meldon Quarry. Outcrops in Crackington Haven and around Bude mark the presence of Upper Carboniferous deposits in the region, the 131 metre cliff at Crackington with its zig-zag folds giving dramatic insight into the powerful forces that have affected the area. The Crackington Formation with shales, thin sandstones, and pebble beds display sedimentary structures characteristic of deep-water turbidites. They were deposited after the movement of sediments down slope into the basinal area; the slope materials having been mobilized either by excessive build up or by Earth movements. The downhill movement produced scouring, and the deposition of higher-density sediments on top of basinal muds resulted in a range of sedimentary structures. At Bude the deposits of thick sandstones with interbedded siltstones and shales indicate shallower-water conditions than those of the Crackington Formation. The discovery of non-marine bivalves in these deposits enables one to correlate them with the Coal Measures of South Wales.

The deposition of shallower-water sediments in the Upper Carboniferous, together with the large- and small-scale structures present in Devon and Cornwall indicate that the Armorican Earth Movement was effective over a long period of time. Complex folds and small thrust planes in various outcrops indicate a north–south shortening of approximately 35–40 per cent. Overturned folds also support the evidence of a major prolonged movement from the south. This movement affected all the various rocks with the younger Carboniferous strata suffering the most.

The great stresses on the crust at the end of the Carboniferous are not only reflected by faults and folds, however, for such occasions in the Earth's history encourage the movement of deep-seated magmas into folded regions. Such was the case in the south-west with the granitic outcrops of Dartmoor, Bodmin Moor, St Austell, Carn Menellis, and Land's End being the surface expression of an enormous deep-seated batholith. This extends from Dartmoor south-westwards beyond the Scilly Isles. The granite forms the rugged tors, set high on the moorland landscapes. It is quartz-rich with large orthoclase feldspar crystals that give it a particularly attractive texture.

The emplacement of the granites affected the country rocks and resulted in a series of metamorphic aureoles around the various outcrops. Compression and themal metamorphism also took place, with slates, phyllites, and extensive mineralization as the products. The importance of the granites, slates, and minerals, including tin and china clay (Fig. 35) to the economic development of the region is well known. The great pyramids of the china clay workings around St Austell and the stark, yet evocative ruins of mine buildings along the coast, bear witness to industries that in some cases began with the Romans.

In post-Carboniferous times the south-west region of England was lifted above sea-level. A continuous cover of red-coloured breccias, conglomerates, and sands rests unconformably on the Carboniferous rocks in the east-north-east of the region, with isolated outcrops in the south, in older strata, being indicative of a greater coverage in earlier geological periods.

Fig. 35. China clay pit at Lee Moor, Dartmoor.

The red rocks of the dunland areas are the products of a terrestrial environment, and their presence enhances the character and colour of an area already noted for its outstanding beauty. In geological terms they denote the erosion of the relict Carboniferous landscape in Permian times.

Evidence of a Cretaceous cover in the south-west exists in the Haldon Hills to the north-east of Teignmouth. Here the beds of sands with chert nodules represent the most south-westerly outliers of the Cretaceous in England and are evidence of overstepping by Cretaceous strata of older rocks. Younger rocks of Tertiary age, including the Oligocene clays and lignites of Bovey Tracey and the Pleistocene cave infill of Kent's Cavern, near Torquay, provide evidence of more recent geological events. To these can be added the structural phenomena imprinted on the region by the forces generated during the Alpine Earth Movement.

A small number of recurring landscape types makes up the scenery of most of the southern half of the south-west peninsula. The high moorland of Dartmoor, reaching 621 metres at High Willhays (see Fig. 36 for locations) is the type example of a granitic upland, and its character is repeated on a smaller scale on Bodmin and St Austell Moors. A second category includes gently rolling plateaux which descend in a series of steps from the uplands, and show a particularly fine development in the South Hams. A third component consists of steep-sided valleys, cutting deeply into the plateaux and then typically terminating in the heads of estuaries. Finally, the southern coastline shows a pattern of bold cliffs, as between Bolt Head and Bolt Tail, deep and narrow estuaries such as that of the Dart, and shallow embayments, as at Bigbury Bay.

The rocks and their arrangement only partly account for this assemblage of landscapes. The scenery of Dartmoor is rather typical of that developed on granitic rocks, so that a visitor familiar with granitic landscapes elsewhere would see at once a family resemblance. Elsewhere, however, undulating plateaux extend indiscriminately over various rock types and structures, and in fact much of Dartmoor itself is made up of partly dissected plateaux. Many of the river valleys show little relationship to geological structure: the Tamar and the Fal, for example, flow across east–west trending structures. On the other hand, the Bovey valley north-east of Haytor is a fine example of a fault-guided feature. It might be expected that the coastline would express an intricate relationship between the character of the rock and the work of the sea. Locally this is true: the most resistant rocks tend to stand out as promontories; for example, tough igneous material underlies Nare Head, and softer rock tends to form embayments, as at Tor Bay, which is developed in relatively weak rocks of Permian age. However, the presence of deep, winding estuaries, and of ancient shorelines now inland, suggests a more complicated story. It is believed that the south-west has reached its present shape by passing through a complex sequence of events, which scientists are still patiently unravelling.

The idea of a complicated history is nowhere better illustrated than on Dartmoor, where the granite landforms of the south-west reach their finest

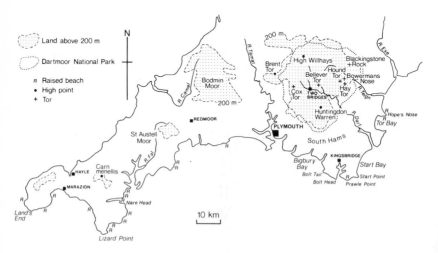

Fig. 36. Location map showing the main features mentioned in the section on land-forms.

1. Looking south from the escarpment of the North Downs at Newlands Corner near Guildford. Chalk scrub occurs on the lower slopes of the escarpment, while the farmland on the lower ground coincides in part with the Gault outcrop. The mainly poor soils of the Lower Greensand country beyond are associated with extensive birchwoods and coniferous plantations.

2. Jurassic sediments of the Boulonnais with cross-stratification and ferruginous lenses. Such deposits and structures are often evidence of shallow-water environments. **3.** Solution pipes in Chalk, northern France. The pipes were etched out by percolating rainwater and infilled by a mixture of limon and reworked Tertiary sediments.

4. View overlooking the Cirque du Fer à Cheval, an embayment within the larger valley of the Ruculée des Planches, north-east of Poligny. The Cirque probably developed by the headward erosion of the river Cuisance which emerges as a spring at the foot of the steep, wooded limestone slopes. **5.** The French–Italian Alps looking north-east from the base of Mont Blanc. Note the frost-shattered ridges and buttresses separated by glaciers, and the wooded lower slopes. The small size of the stream and the coarse channel debris suggests great seasonal variations in discharge. The protective wall and the vegetated area of river gravel to the left support this view.

6. Polished and grooved rock surface in the valley of the Dora Baltea, suggestive of glacial abrasion. 7. Morainic landscape around Llyn Idwal. Fresh late-glacial moraines in the middle distance contrast with an older, smoother, terminal moraine in the background.

8. Fossil-ripple marks in Lower Palaeozoic rocks of the Capel Curig region of Snowdonia, which like those of the Ffestionog Grits are indicative of a shallow-water environment. **9.** Heathland dominated by common heather or ling, the New Forest.

10. A granitic tor of south-west England. The term was originally used in this region to describe residual rock masses that invariably cap hills. **11.** Volcanic landscapes of the northern Chaîne des Puys, seen from the slopes of the Puy-de-Dôme. The partly wooded puys in the distance contrast with the barren scene in the foreground. Note the fresh, unaltered nature of the scenery, which has experienced little erosion since the volcanic episode.

12. View from the west-facing slope of the Puy-de-Dôme showing typical landscape elements of the Auvergne. In the foreground abandoned pasture had been invaded by scrub, which gives way to areas of afforestation and small fields. Extensive communal grazings can be seen in the distance. **13.** Unconformable junction between strongly deformed basement rocks and overlying Tertiary boulder bed, exposed at the southern end of Playa de Pals, Costa Brava.

14. A view up the valley of the River Llobregat. The river flows to the north of Montserrat and cuts through a thick succession of Cainozoic conglomerates and sandstones. The waterfall occurs approximately 100 metres west of a major thrust plane and just above the junction between Cainozoic and Mesozoic rocks. **15.** A view towards the so-called Camel Rock of the Montserrat mountains. Note the rounded form of the upper slopes which is due to a combination of massive bedding, vertical jointing, and erosion.

expression. Here the landscape is typically made up of an assemblage of upstanding rocky peaks or tors, spreads of bouldery debris, long, gently curving slopes, shallow, boggy depressions, and infrequent, deep valleys.

Within Dartmoor the area around Haytor, east of Widecombe, offers many indicators as to how the landscape has evolved. Haytor is made up of two components, Haytor East and Haytor West, which are separated by a zone of low ground, referred to as an avenue. Such avenues are quite common features of the Dartmoor tors; one of the best examples divides Hound tor, which lies north-west of Haytor, into two units. The face of Haytor East, seen from the avenue, is crossed by major planes of weakness, or joints, which can be observed to run both horizontally and vertically. The relatively closely spaced horizontal joints may be a result of the release of immense pressures, as rocks overlying the intruded granite were steadily worn away. On the other hand, the vertical joints may have resulted from either tensional or shearing forces, set up when the granite was being emplaced. The arrangement of these joints gives a blocky or squared appearance to Haytor East. The form of Haytor West, on the other hand, is controlled by joints that are sloping at a pronounced angle.

This principle, that the arrangement of the planes of weakness determines the shapes of tors, can be widely applied on Dartmoor. Bowerman's Nose, 2 kilometres north of Hound tor, has an impressive tower-like appearance, the result of pronounced vertical jointing. When the chief joints are arranged horizontally a squat, table-like shape is the result. This is well displayed by Bellever tor, south of Postbridge. Occasionally the joints show a marked slope, and in this situation the tor may have a domed shape. Blackingstone Rock, east of Moreton Hamstead, is a good illustration of this circumstance. It is well worth bearing this principle in mind when examining other Dartmoor tors.

There is, therefore, quite a good relationship between the form of the tors and the structure of the constituent granite. However, rain and perhaps frost are steadily attacking the rock, moulding it into shapes that are much less controlled by geological characteristics. Because rainwater takes up carbon dioxide from the atmosphere it is slightly acid, and so it quite readily attacks the weaker minerals in the granite. The result is a softening and rounding of the tor outline, with the occasional development of nearly circular depressions on flat surfaces. This smoothing effect, which can be seen towards the summit of Haytor East, is often most pronounced on the side facing west, which is the main direction of rain-bearing winds. A local expert has asserted that in foggy weather a tor may be used as a compass, as its most rounded side points to the west.

There is good evidence that corrosion has not been the only process at work on the Dartmoor granite. Many tors are surrounded by extensive spreads of rock debris called clitters, which typically rest on gentle gradients. They are the result of very cold conditions when water seeped into granite joints, froze, and so shattered the rock. A close examination of the tors normally fails to reveal any evidence that this process is happening today, and so it is believed that the clitters were largely formed during the last cold episode of the Quaternary Ice Age, called the Devensian. The ice that periodically mantled much of Britain failed to advance as far as Dartmoor, which nevertheless experienced an arctic climate when ice sheets lay just to the north.

While the clitters are the debris resulting from frost shattering, this process also affected the shapes of some tors, together with their immediate surroundings. In particular, frost action may have brought about the feature known as a rock shelter, or overhang. By walking round Haytor West one can see that the base of the tor has been undercut. This is the result of frost selectively attacking the lower granite (which yields readily since it possesses many closely spaced joints) and making little headway in the upper granite, whose joints are much further apart. A large-scale illustration of the work that can be carried out by freezing and thawing can be seen in western Dartmoor, in the vicinity of Cox Tor. This tor is made of rock that has been altered by the intense heat and pressures that were set up when the granite was first intruded. The attack by frost during the cold episodes of the Ice Age has produced a striking sequence of step-like terraces that partly surround the tor, like ancient and degraded earthworks. The precise way in which these land-forms were produced is still a mystery. The avenue is an equally controversial feature. It has been suggested that it may have originated in the weakened central part of a local dome in the granite, opened up by frost action that was readily able to exploit the closely jointed rock. Blackingstone Rock may represent an early stage, and the avenue between East and West Haytors a later stage.

These three themes of rock character, frost shattering, and steady erosion by rain-water underlie most of the attempts that scientists have made to understand how the granite landscapes of the south-west came into existence. An immediate clue to their relative importance occurs in a quarry opened up in a shallow depression north-east of Haytor East. Here the spacing between the joints varies from 0.3 metres to 2.0 metres, while inspection of the face of the main tor shows that joint separation there is 2–4 metres. The depressions of the granite landscape may simply be areas where the rock is more susceptible to destruction by water because of its close joint spacing, while the tors are upstanding features because they have fewer weaknesses for water to penetrate.

Argument has centred about the mechanism by which water has done its work. Some investigators have emphasized the importance of freezing and thawing, and have suggested that the tor landscape is relatively recent. According to this view the landscape has been etched out during the last two million years by selective frost action, controlled by joint spacing. Other scientists have disagreed, and have favoured the theory of selective rotting by weakly acid rainwater the process still, however, being controlled by joint density. They have used as evidence the quarry at Two Bridges (Fig. 37) where, they say, a tor of sound rock can actually be seen in the process of emerging from a surrounding mass of deeply rotted granite. They suggest that the process of selective corrosion of the granite may have been going on for some fifty million years, and the effect of the Ice Age was merely to add some detail, such as the clitter, to an already recognizable landscape. These barren granite moorlands, with their mysterious tors, are still the subject of keen debate.

Tors are eye-catching, dramatic features, frequently associated with a second, less striking type of land-form which may offer a significant clue towards the earlier history of the landscape. A glance at a map of southern Dartmoor shows that many of the summits reach a remarkably similar height. Pupers Hill (464 metres), Huntingdon Warren (473 metres), Nakes Hill (488 metres) and Snowdon (493 metres) are believed to be part of a formerly extensive, gently undulating plain, which varies in height between 463 metres and 493 metres. A similar surface, rather more fragmentary in character, may be identified in northern Dartmoor, where it ranges in height between 518 metres and 579 metres. The Dart basin separates these two surfaces, which may have been originally continuous. The original feature was tilted gently to the south during the middle Tertiary.

This theme is repeated at varying heights throughout the south-west

Fig. 37. Old quarry in granite near Two Bridges, Dartmoor. The sound granite on the left could emerge as a tor when the rotted material on the right has been removed by erosion.

peninsula. Of particular note is the occurence of surfaces within the general height ranges 266–304 metres, and 222–250 metres. Fragments of the higher level can be seen in the Tamar basin, where, for example, the volcanic mass of Brent Tor reaches 344 metres. Both levels are well developed on Bodmin Moor, while the lower surface is clearly seen on Culm Measures around the Tamar headwaters, and on the Carnmenellis and Land's End granites in west Cornwall. Even clearer plateaux with heights between 122 metres and 152 metres may be seen in the area of the South Hams.

Careful observation has suggested, then, that an important component in the landscape of south-west England is a staircase-like arrangement of largely unwarped plateaux, which truncate the underlying rocks irrespective of their resistance or arrangement. These are examples of planation surfaces, which we have already described for the Jura. A popular explanation for many of these surfaces is that they were planed off by the sea, then well above its present level. This may be the correct explanation as far as the lower surfaces are concerned but research has shown that the higher surfaces, including those of Dartmoor, were probably fashioned by the same agents of erosion that are wearing down the landscape today. Of course, the older and higher surfaces were probably formed under a climate quite different from that of the present day, and at a time when the sea-level was higher. There has been much support for the view that they were formed under a hot, humid, tropical climate during the earlier part of the Tertiary period.

Although the planation surfaces are an important part of the landscape, they are often strongly dissected by river valleys. The character of individual valleys, and the patterns made when many streams are investigated, provide evidence for various episodes in river development. Valley sides of the streams flowing from Dartmoor have relatively gentle upper slopes which steepen markedly as the river channel is approached. This suggests that the streams have incised their valleys with increasing rapidity. The occurrence of terraces, such as those of the River Dart, hints at episodes when the rate of down-cutting slowed markedly. The stream pattern of the region is dominated by south-flowing systems, such as those of the Exe, Teign, Tamar, and Fal. This orientation may be a result of the gentle southerly tilt which occurred during the middle Tertiary, and which favoured, for example, the south-flowing tributaries of the Dart system. However, this relatively simple arrangement was occasionally altered, as the new rivers responded to local circumstances. This theme is well displayed in west Cornwall. The original southward-flowing drainage was reversed in the Hayle-Marazion depression, and the present course of the Camel suggests that the original line flowed to the south, via Red Moor. The early systems have been altered through the erosive action of vigorous streams draining to the north-west coast.

The final, and in many ways most striking, landscape unit of the south-west is its coastline. This partly reflects the control exercised by rock type and arrangement. For example, Bigbury Bay and Start Bay may have originated as basins of Permian Age, filled with relatively weak breccias and sandstones, which have been comparatively easily eroded. They contrast with the intervening zone of resistant metamorphic rocks (schists) which make up the fine cliffed coast between Bolt Tail and Start Point, the site of so many shipwrecks over the centuries.

The coast is not, however, merely a zone where rocks respond in various ways to marine erosion. It has passed through a complicated series of events, largely relating to the two million years of the Ice Age. The evidence for this is quite well preserved, and is of various types.

A first, typical component is that of a raised, step-like feature, often mantled by beach deposits (Fig. 38) and which stands well above the present sea-level. This feature is well preserved on the harder rocks, such as on the resistant schists between Hallsands and Splat Cove. Here three distinct levels can be distinguished: the modern wave-cut platform, and two benches which now stand approximately 2 metres and 4 metres above high water. These features are clearly seen in Lannacombe Bay, just west of Start Point. Further north the old village of Hallsands, now destroyed, was built upon a quartz–mica schist bench at about 4 metres above high water. A further bench standing at approximately 7 metres can be traced along the coast between Prawle Point and Splat Cove on the western side of the Kingsbridge estuary. This platform is a convincing example of the way in which wave-cut

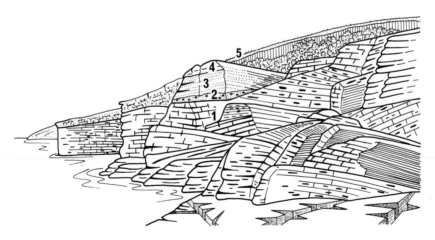

Fig. 38. The Hope's Nose raised beach, Torquay. The raised beach rests on an old wave cut platform (1) at 7·3 metres above high tide. The beach is made up of a basement bed (2) 0·3 to 0·4 metres thick and made up of coarse local material. Above is a sand (3) up to 3·7 metres thick and cemented by carbonate of lime overlain by 0·6 to 0·9 metres of loose blown sand (4). The top deposit (5) consists of recent hill wash. This raised beach was laid down during the last interglacial.

benches typically truncate geological structures. It cuts across the quartz–mica schist and hornblende–chlorite schist in the Prawle and Rockhern areas, paying no attention to the arrangement of the rocks. Although these platforms are now being destroyed by the sea, which is attacking them along steeply sloping planes of weakness, they nevertheless provide clear signs of changes in sea-level.

These ancient marine platforms are frequently mantled by an unconsolidated deposit, which contains many angular fragments, and which is called head. The origin of this term is obscure but the material itself offers important evidence regarding the nature of the climate during the cold episodes of the Ice Age.

Head deposits are finely exposed between Great Matchcombe Sands and Prawle Point, in cliffs up to 30 metres high. Locally the head has slumped over beach material of much more recent age. The bulk of the deposit is made up of relatively fine-grained material which is reddish-brown in colour, although variations do occur from light grey and yellow to sepia and black. A close inspection suggests that the head always originates locally. For example, in the Torbay and Plymouth areas the head consists mainly of limestone fragments, while adjacent to the schist uplands it is made up of that rock type. More detailed observations have shown that the larger fragments have their long-axes oriented downslope.

The evidence of raised platforms and the head suggests that the following events affected the coastline of Devon and Cornwall during the Ice Age. During the interglacial periods when the Earth's glaciers had shrunk, sea-level was higher than it is today, and wave activity cut one or more benches. These are occasionally still mantled with beach shingle as at Hope's Nose in Tor Bay. The subsequent glacial periods saw a fall in the level of the oceans as water became locked up in the form of ice. During this time the south-west peninsula probably lay just south of the southern-most British ice-sheet, and intense freezing and thawing occurred under an arctic climate. Easily broken rock was shattered and sludged down slope to form the head. The end of the last glacial episode saw a recovery of sea-level and a flooding of the coastline to produce the magnificent estuaries that are such an attractive feature of south Devon and Cornwall.

The vegetation of Devon and Cornwall makes a distinctive contribution to the scenic beauty for which these counties are famed, and displays contrasts which harmonize closely with the fabric of the physical setting. Thus, the isolated granite masses, together with the serpentine of the Lizard, give rise, for the major part, to open, sometimes quite rugged moors and heathland. Over the intervening plateaux, developed across the slates, grits, and sandstones on the southern flank of the Devon synclinorium, the landscape is very different and typically comprises a patchwork of small fields and hedges, traversed by sunken lanes. Although the crowding hedgerows tend to convey the impression of a well-wooded environment, such woods as do exist are generally confined to the valleys dissecting the plateaux, especially those opening south into the English Channel. The coast itself provides yet a third vegetation component, and the least altered wildlife habitats.

Formerly much, if not all, of the region was forested, possibly up to and including the summit of Dartmoor. Pollen analysis has revealed that woodland destruction on Dartmoor began soon after 3000 BC, with the arrival of Neolithic farmers in the area. The destruction accelerated in the following Bronze Age, and by the subsequent Iron Age moorland had largely replaced forest. Even so the character of the vegetation of present-day Dartmoor owes more to the impact of man and his animals throughout the historical period, and not least in the recent past. A few vestigial fragments of degraded oakwood do, in fact, survive as reminders of the once-extensive forest cover, in the upper reaches of the more remote valleys of Dartmoor. Here the trees grow among a protective clitter. The highest parts of the moor, however, perhaps amounting to half the total area, now support blanket bog, growing on thick peat. Bog moss, the deciduous purple moor grass – which is actually a pale straw-colour for much of the year – along with heather and sedges are the dominant plants. The initial growth of peat was triggered by the deterioration of the soil ecosystem that resulted from the original phase of woodland destruction. The latter was achieved by the combined effects of burning and grazing, which thereafter on the wet, higher ground maintained conditions favourable to more or less continuous peat accumulation. Paradoxically, these same land-use activities seem now to be primarily responsible for the contemporary widespread erosive dissection, or 'hagging' of the peat. Hagging eventually leads to impassable terrain and affects the quality of water supply in the catchments concerned.

On the slopes surrounding the two central blocks of wet moor, dry heaths and grassland prevail. The heaths carry heather and, to a much smaller extent, bilberry. They have diminished in extent in recent times because of over-frequent burning or 'swaling', and there has been a corresponding increase of grassland. This is actually a familiar trend in the ecology of upland Britain, as was shown in the case of Snowdonia. Similarly, within the grassland there has been an increase of poorer pasture species such as mat grass, but their spread has been inhibited to a degree by the above-average diversity of grazing stock, including cattle and horses as well as sheep. There is, nevertheless, progressive bracken infestation of both the heaths and grassland. On the heaths this is due largely to the influence of burning, for when this takes place early in the year, with a view to eliminating old, woody heather, the bracken fronds have not emerged. The grasslands, on the other hand, are not deliberately fired. The spread of bracken in this community, therefore, is partly for the reason that the plant is no longer cut for animal bedding and, more importantly, because sheep graze areas so closely that cattle, which are capable of holding bracken in check by 'treading', avoid them. In the grasslands on the periphery of Dartmoor there is also some gorse, a plant which can provide nutritious winter feed, although yet again numerous fires appear to have greatly reduced its frequency.

Collectively then, peat erosion, deterioration of pasture, and bracken infestation indicate that in ecological terms Dartmoor may be described as a wasting resource. Interestingly, a start on afforestation, which is a more productive use of the land and one which need not be aesthetically unappealing, was made in the eighteenth century. Despite the long interval since then, there is surprisingly little commercial timber on this vast tract of marginal land, and the same is true of the other granite outcrops now to be considered.

The vegetation of Bodmin Moor differs principally from that of Dartmoor in that bog vegetation is highly restricted. Communities of bog moss are found only in very wet spots known locally as piskie pits. The majority of the moor carries damp grassland chiefly of purple moor grass with variable admixtures of heather and rushes. On the drier, less peaty soils better quality fescue–bent pastures are found. Further south, the Hensbarrow and Carnmenellis granites have been extensively scarred by mining activity, and there has also been much enclosure of land for cottage cultivation, so that few representative tracts of the earlier heathlands remain. Continuous heathlands are next met on the granites of Land's End and on the serpentine-rich rocks of the Lizard. Those of the Lizard are especially noteworthy, for over a sizeable part of them the lilac-flowered Cornish heath flourishes, together with numerous other plants of south-west European affinity which in Britain are either restricted to this part of Cornwall or are rarely found elsewhere. Another unusual feature of these heaths is that lime-hating, or calcifuge plants like common heather or ling, and bell heather, grow side-by-side with calcicoles such as the dropwort and ladies bedstraw, plants which are typical of more alkaline base-rich soils. The explanation of this apparent anomaly lies in the chemical composition of serpentine, for while it is lime-deficient, it contains enough other bases like magnesium to counteract any tendency towards significant soil acidification.

The agrarian, essentially pastoral countryside that separates the moors and heathland is more obviously the product of man's activities. Field patterns dating from the Bronze and Iron Ages are still clearly evident in Cornwall and Devon, and probably all but a few of the region's farms were established by 1350. Around the larger hamlets and villages at this time much of the land was unenclosed and divided into strips which were owned in common by the farming community. However, the decline in population and the consequent shortage of men to plough the land following the Black Death of 1348 caused much of the open land to be put down to pasture. To control grazing on the new pasture, hedges were planted around many of the former individual strips, and in this fossilized form they are still widespread in Devon and Cornwall. The demand for wool by the expanding Tudor cloth industry reinforced the changeover from arable to grass, so that by the end of the sixteenth century much of the farmland of the two counties was enclosed. In the rest of England, the enclosure movement was to reach its zenith much later, in the eighteenth century.

The demand for wool, and for food for the expanding settlements associated with mining, quarrying, and the ports, gave the impetus for the enclosure of what hitherto had been waste land. In many instances elongated roadside strips and rough ground around communities connected with quarrying, mining, and the woollen industry were transformed into new fields and smallholdings by cottagers. On a larger scale still, numerous fields were added to existing farms by encroachment on to the adjoining moor and heath. Apart from their location, these late additions to the landscape may be distinguished by their generally straight-sided form. Since the last war a major trend in British farming has been the enlargement of fields by hedge-row removal to permit the use of larger, more efficient machines. The effects in Devon and Cornwall have not been dramatic, however, since the rural economy is still based chiefly on livestock. In other words the incentive to remove hedges is lessened, for they still serve their original functions as stock-proof farm boundaries and as boundaries for internal grazing management.

The woodland scattered across the agricultural landscapes falls into two basic categories. By far the most numerous are the 'coppice-with-standards' oakwoods of the steeper valley sides, sites unsuited to clearance for either arable or livestock farming. Such woods were once an integral part of the rural economy. The trees, or standards, were either planted or allowed to regenerate naturally at a density of roughly 50 per hectare, and were subsequently felled on an 80–100-year cycle. At these comparatively low densities competition between the trees for light was limited and so they characteristically developed a 'stag-horn' branching habit at trunk heights of only 6–7 metres. In this way a plentiful supply of 'knee pieces' and 'angle joints' was ensured for the construction of timber-framed houses and wooden ships. Oak bark for the tanning of leather was also obtained in large quantities. Hazel was able to thrive in the light shade beneath the oaks and was 'coppiced' or cut to the base on an 8–10-year rotation to provide fencing material, bean sticks, hurdles, and wattle, the latter being widely used in the construction of traditional wattle-and-daub walls. After coppicing, sheets of spring flowers such as bluebell, anemone, and primrose were much in evidence, responding to the additional light admitted to the woodland floor, but as the hazel shrubs regenerated from the stump or 'stool', these rather shade-intolerant flowers became progressively less conspicuous. The coppice-with-standards system of woodland management ceased to be economically viable after about 1860, for it was highly labour intensive and the demand for timber in any case changed in favour of cheap, imported softwood. Hence today these woodlands are essentially neglected, unless there is management for wildlife conservation or more intensive methods of hardwood production which have been recently introduced. Despite losing many of the characteristics referred to above, however, the woods are of immense ecological value, since they often grow on sites which have never been given over to other land uses, and have thus provided a continuous habitat for the survival of woodland species. Ecologically they may be defined as primary woodlands.

The reorganization of the English countryside in the eighteenth and early nineteenth centuries also resulted in the creation of much secondary woodland, when land around country houses was planted with many species of trees, mainly hardwoods, but also several softwoods. Although primarily intended as productive plantations, they were laid out in such a way as to generate an informal scene of great aesthetic interest and charm. Often they formed part of a larger plan or design for the estate around a country house, drawn up by the great landscape architects of the time, such as 'Capability' Brown, Repton, and Kent. Good examples of such wooded landscapes can be seen around Luscombe House in Devon and Antony House in Cornwall. Unfortunately much of the landscaping around Saltram, near Plymouth, has been spoiled by subsequent urban and industrial development. More recently the Forestry Commission, the Duchy of Cornwall, and private landowners have established essentially coniferous plantations, and though individually they tend to be larger than the earlier broadleaved woods, their combined area is much smaller.

The maritime vegetation of the coast adds further diversification to the landscape of west Devon and Cornwall. Sand-dune systems, known locally as towans or meols, are particularly well developed along the Atlantic coast, at Bude, Padstow, Penhole Sands, Godrevy Towan, and Upton Towan. Their formation generally followed a similar pattern. Near the sea specialized, salt-tolerant, summer annuals are able to survive among the flotsam and jetsam of the high-water mark. They trap blown sand and cause the build-up of a small dune feature, which less saline grasses such as sand couch grass and, later, marram grass can colonize. These much larger, perennial plants trap blown sand even more effectively so that a line of much higher dunes accumulates. The high dunes are relatively mobile under the influence of the prevailing wind and so move inland. Periodically small, U-shaped dunes bud off from the main ridge of sand and migrate snout-first leaving behind a 'blow-out'. These snouts migrate more rapidly than the wings of the newly formed secondary dunes, because they are higher and therefore less easily colonized and stabilized by vegetation. Eventually these U-shaped dunes advance on to older dune-ridges further inland, which will also have suffered blow-outs. The resulting terrain has a very confused, chaotic appearance. Beyond the high, mobile dunes the relief is lower and the sand is more or less stabilized by a cover of vegetation, usually dune pasture with much bracken which passes in turn into dune scrub. Between the broken dune-ridges and within some of the larger U-shaped secondary dunes, hollows, or slacks, are often eroded down to the water-table. Here, where the wet sand is too heavy to be blown along, are found associations of plants which vary with the salinity of the water. Near the sea typical maritime species such as sea rocket and the sand wort are common, whereas inland dwarf willow, rush communities, and damp pasture are prominent. In recent times the inherent instability of the dune system has been increased by recreation pressure, for wherever the plant cover is appreciably disturbed or eroded then sand can be remobilized.

Finally, the coastal cliffs above the high-water mark also display a variety of plant life. Where the influence of spray is marked the plants are mainly very salt-tolerant, but above this the vegetation is transitional to the grass-land or heath of the cliff-top. Depending on exposure and wave action the cliff vegetation descends to within 6 metres of the high-water mark, and, in sheltered coves, to the high-tide level.

If any single landscape theme impresses the visitor to the south-west, it must be that of diversity, resulting from the great variety of rock types, the range of erosional agents that carved the scenery, and the complex series of modifications carried out by Man on the original natural vegetation. This theme of diversity is enhanced by the intricacy and variation of the coastline.

The landscapes we see are the result of both natural and human processes. During the Tertiary the region was periodically planed by various erosional agents and intermittently disturbed by Earth movements. But during the brief Quaternary, the landscape experienced the full rigours of frost-based processes. The final shaping of the tors may have been completed at this time, together with clitter deposition. The warming post-glacial climate saw the widespread development of forest, soon to be cleared by Neolithic farmers. The granite uplands degenerated to moorland and bog, while the more fertile marginal zones were farmed as early as the 1300s. The lower plateaux which cut across largely sedimentary rocks now show what, for many visitors, is the typical Devon landscape: a mosaic of small hedge-bounded fields crossed by a maze of sunken lanes.

Variety, then, is the keynote of the south-west, expressed both in the range of geological materials and in the diversity of the landscapes that have been developed on them.

5 The northern volcanic province of the Massif Central

The Massif Central (Fig. 39) provides the setting for a more detailed investigation of the volcanic province of the Chaîne des Puys and Mont Dore. It is a vast upland region, covering approximately one-sixth of all France. Within this extensive territory there are rugged peaks, deep-glaciated valleys, and large stretches of flat or gently inclined plateaux. The journey south from Paris to this area crosses essentially the same geological features as the journey towards the Mediterranean described in Chapter 1. The sediments of the Jurassic aureole overstep the ancient Precambrian basement of the Massif, north of Culan, on the main Chateauroux–Clermont-Ferrand road. The lovely Chateau of Culan is actually sited on basement rocks, and a small quarry opposite on the main road offers the first opportunity of studying the rocks that form the foundations of the Massif. Here the basement is represented by mica schists and gneisses of the Lémovico-Arverne metamorphic subdivision. This last corresponds roughly with the Limousin and Auvergne regions, with the former referring to the plateaux which form the northern and western areas of the Massif. The most northerly of these is termed the Marche, and the metamorphics of Culan form the north-east corner of this area.

Outcrops of metamorphic rocks occur intermittently on the roadside from Culan to a point approximately 6 kilometres north of Montluçon, where the great north-east–south-west trending Boussac fault marks the contact between them and an alkaline granite. Granite rocks, as in the Massif de la Serre, are a major component of the basement, or *socle*, and radiometric dating indicates that the majority of those in the Massif were intruded around the middle of the Carboniferous period.

South of the Boussac fault, towards the spa of Néris-les-Bains you will notice that the granite rocks give rise to gently undulating countryside. A few kilometres before Néris, however, your view south is restricted by the appearance of a distinct scarp. This marks the outcrop of the Mont Marault granite which forms the high plateau on which the spa, famed for its thermal baths, sits. The plateau extends from Néris to Montaigut, where the granite is faulted against basement rocks. The N143 from Montaigut to St Eloy drops rather steeply as you enter the last hamlet and the steep slope, together with the appearance of a number of coal mines, should provoke some questions. On the immediate outskirts of St Eloy it is possible to look back at the scarp and observe that it extends for many kilometres in a north-east to south-west direction. Notice how the scarp front is divided into nearly triangular facets by the incision of streams draining across it. You can also see that additional coal mines and tips extend far to the south and that from a topographic viewpoint the coal-bearing strata occur below the basement rocks. The north-east to south-west feature represents the line of the great Carboniferous furrow, the Sillon Houiller. The latter consists of a long, straight fault zone that extends for approximately 250 kilometres from La Crésigne in the south-west to Noyant in the north-east. It is both narrow and sub-vertical, and is uniquely characterized by the presence of small coal basins. The coal is of Upper Carboniferous age and was preserved when the Sillon acted as a normal graben during the Hercynian Orogeny.

A limited exposure of coal measure shales and basal conglomerate sits directly on basement rocks. A collection of pebbles from the conglomerate will show you that the majority are of mica schists, gneisses, granites, and vein quartz and that the boundary itself is unconformable. The conglomerates and shales are tilted almost to the vertical and you can therefore conclude that their present position is a result of post-depositional movements.

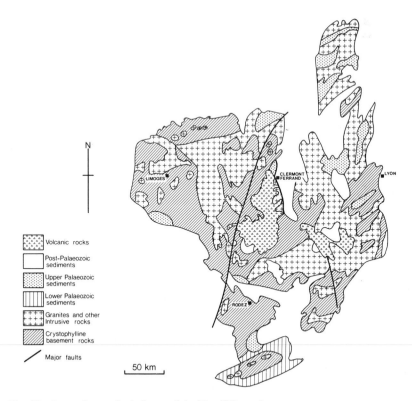

Fig. 39. An outline geological map of the Massif Central.

Basement gneisses and schists form the south-eastern margin of the St Eloy vally and the rugged highlands of the Pont de Menat synform. Excellent exposures of the basement series may be studied between Pont de Menat and the thermal spa of Chateauneuf les Bains. This section cuts across the south-eastern region of the synform which, although complex, is extremely interesting. The traverse should not be attempted without the regional guide, but taken slowly it provides you with a clear insight of the petrological and structural history of the basement series. The scenery of the area towards Chateauneuf is dominated by high-level, undulating plateaux that cut indiscriminately across the underlying rocks and are part of an early Tertiary erosion surface. As a result of subsequent regional uplift, the River Sioule has incised its channel to produce a spectacular series of gorges. A fine example of a meandering valley which, through time, has been incised into the underlying country rock can be seen from a vantage point about 3.5 kilometres east of Chateauneuf, on D227.

At Menat itself, a small basinal structure infilled with bituminous shales occurs within the basement complex. The shales were deposited over sixty million years ago and the discovery of the fossils of numerous insects, fish, and other vertebrates as well as a host of plants indicates that the area was once the site of a small forest-bounded lake. The shales are of Palaeocene age and are the oldest recorded Tertiary rocks within the Massif Central. Permission to collect from this locality is restricted, but if you succeed in obtaining a permit from the local Mayor, many rewarding hours can be spent splitting the finely varved shales in the search for the elusive fossil of a turtle or small mammal.

From Menat to just beyond Combrande, the basement rocks again present a rugged landscape. Nearer Riom, however, it is possible to observe the lowlands of the Limagne Basin to the south-east and the peaks of the Chaîne des Puys to the immediate south. The junction between the basement and the Tertiary sediments of the Limagne follows a fault, and evidence for this exists in a sharp break of slope. To the east of Riom the fault splits into two and evidence of a major fracture zone exists 250 metres to the west of the depression of St Hippolyte. At this locality the granitoid rocks, which rise high over the plain to the east, are broken and shattered and veins rich in fluorite, barytes, quartz, and galena criss-cross a massive fault breccia.

At St Hippolyte (Fig. 40) a distinct fertile depression occurs at the foot of the granitoid mass, and a closer investigation of the materials within the structure suggests that they were waterlain. The coarse-grained sediments contain pebbles of granites, volcanic lavas, and derived fragments of Oligocene algal colonies and trace fossils. The sediments were therefore deposited in post-Oligocene times and their unconsolidated nature, together with the fresh volcanic fragments, suggest that both depression and infill are relatively recent phenomena. Having seen the huge cones of the Chaîne des Puys to the south it is not unreasonable for us to link the St Hippolyte depression with recent volcanic activity. In fact the depression is thought to

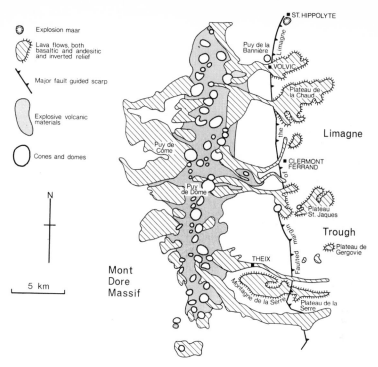

Fig. 40. A geological map of the Chaîne des Puys and environs showing the major cones and lava flows. Note the alignment of the cones and domes that make up the Chaîne and the way they parallel the Limagne Fault. The associated lava flows typically give rise to inverted relief as they extend into the Limagne Trough.

represent an explosive event that actually took place during the Holocene epoch. (This theme is developed in the section on scenery.) From St Hippolyte you can follow the line of the great Limagne border fault south along the road to Volvic. To the west of the road the basement rocks form steep cliffs, while to the east the flat lowlands of the basin stretch for many kilometres. Just before Volvic a short detour up to the Chateau de Tournoël, perched high above the lowlands, will prove most rewarding. Here the steeply inclined materials that form the eastern slopes of the Puy de la Bannière can be studied. A small quarry to the left of the road as one ascends, and just below the Chateau, presents a fresh section and when handling the cindery materials you will soon appreciate that they are the air-fall products of a once-active volcano (Fig. 41). Their colour reflects both the original rock type and also its subsequent weathering, and is discussed in the section on scenery. The majority are irregular in shape and vesicular in nature and are known as scoria, or cinders. A few have a more-aerodynamic shape, however, and such 'bombs' represent lumps of once plastic ejecta that were modified during flight. Other fragments envelop pieces of the

99

Fig. 41. Volcanic bombs are common amongst the pyroclastic rocks of both the Chaînes and the Olot region. Pyroclastic rocks are produced when volcanic materials are thrown into the atmosphere. Bombs result from a lump of liquid lava being spun through the air.

original granitic country rock and from these it is possible to ascertain that the nearby vent of the Puy de la Bannière cut through the basement series.

From the Chateau de Tournoël it is possible to observe that the Puy de la Bannière is very close to the line of the Limagne border fault. It is also an ideal spot on which to reflect on the crustal weaknesses within the area that encouraged the breakthrough of igneous materials. Towards Volvic a further expression of igneous activity is immediately noticeable, for a thick lava flow that extends across both crystalline basement and basinal sediments forms a distinct plateau. Similar flows occur intermittently as far south as Aydat and in some cases it is obvious that the flow direction is controlled by topography. Both the flows and the cones are the products of a volcanic episode that lasted approximately 35 000 years with the most recent event dated by the radiocarbon technique at approximately 1000 AD.

The flows are basaltic in composition and their source or sources can be traced westwards to some of the most spectacular cones of the Chaîne des Puys (Plate 11). The Chaîne consists of some eighty or so cones, many of which you can observe from the summit of the Puy de Dôme (1465 metres). The view to the north is perhaps the more informative and with the aid of a topographic map it is possible to distinguish between various types of volcano by their shape alone. (This theme is developed in the section on land-forms.)

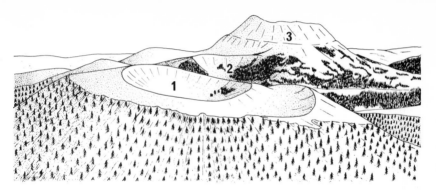

Fig. 42. An aerial view of part of the Chaîne des Puys from north-west to south-east showing the cone-within-cone form of the Puy de Côme (1); open-mouthed crater (2); and the Puy de Dôme (3).

The great cones of the Chaîne des Puys (Fig. 42), together with the lava flows and cinder deposits, are obvious indications of major crustal unrest in this region in recent times. The distribution of the cones coincides with a major north–south basement anticline which was disturbed and fractured during the final phases of the Alpine Orogeny. Violent eruptions were commonplace and a fuller appreciation of the Earth's dynamic forces can be obtained by visits to the explosion craters (maars) of Beaunit and Narse d'Espinasse. Generally these can be compared with the superb crater lakes or calderas of Pavin and Chauvet, although these features lie outside the Chaîne, within the region known as the Massif Mont Dore. This region together with the sister Massif – the Cantal – contains the highest peaks in the Auvergne. They are due to the fact that the basement rocks were tilted upwards, as a result of mid-Tertiary movements, and subsequently covered by a great thickness of volcanic rocks.

Vulcanicity in the Mont Dore and Cantal regions began in the Miocene and reached a peak during the Pliocene epoch. The scale of the two regions is quite staggering: the Massif Mont Dore covers 800 square kilometres and the Cantal volcano has a diameter of some 80 kilometres. The Massif Mont Dore is a complex stratovolcano, where a strip of basement has been broken and downfaulted. The resultant graben was then infilled with ashes and thick lava flows which formed the *planèze* surfaces below La Banne d'Ordanche and Pallaret. The Puy Sancy is the centre of the Massif and its peak, laced with intrusions of resistant acidic rocks, rises to 1886 metres.

A journey from the village of Perrier, to the west of Issoire on the N9, to Mont Dore and Sancy covers most of the phenomena of the Massif. At Perrier it is possible to visit the ancient homes of troglodytes and, within the caves carved into the hillside, study the fabric and composition of mammal-bearing conglomerates and the lahars that rest upon them (Fig. 43).

Fig. 43. Old mud-flow or lahar, near Perrier. The flow is largely made up of volcanic ash together with large blocks of lava. It rests on rounded river gravels.

Just beyond Perrier, westwards, a thick lava flow caps the Plateau de Perrier. The flow is basaltic and locally exhibits excellent columnar cooling joints. It has been dated as Lower Pliocene and therefore it is much older than the 'Couze Chambon' flow which is first encountered at the village of Champaix. This flow is of Pleistocene age and it is possible for you to trace it as far as Murol 12 kilometres to the west. Numerous outcrops show that the flow rests on granitic rocks of the *socle*. It has made an important contribution to the development of the scenery, details of this are given in the section on land-forms. Beyond Chambon the road to Mont Dore climbs high over rocks of the basement complex and on to the volcanics of the central complex. Views from either the top of Puy Gros or the Puy de l'Angle offer beautiful panoramas of the Sancy peaks and of the *planèze* surfaces of Montagne de Bozat and the Plateau des Rigglets. From Puy Sancy the views are even more spectacular and it is possible to sketch or photograph many phenomena and observe the distant peaks of the Cantal and even the Alps.

Like the Massif Mont Dore the Cantal is also a stratovolcano. It is less complex, however, as the relatively straightforward succession of volcanic rocks can be traced from the outlying basement areas, such as Riom lès Montagnes to the central region of Puy Mary. The geology and the scenery of the Cantal is amongst the most spectacular in Europe and excursions within the region should include visits to the volcano-sedimentary section of Cheylade, the rock of Bonnevie in Murat, and Puy Mary. The first of these relates a story of alternating sedimentation and volcanic activity, with Miocene sands resting directly on the basement. The section totals some 200 metres and is capped by a plateau lava of late Pleistocene age, which was dated by the discovery of a Villafranchian flora in the sediments directly below it. The rock of Bonnevie is a volcanic plug which dominates the town of Murat; its beautifully slender prisms providing a spectacular plinth for a gigantic statue of the Virgin Mary. Visitors to the region must be sure to pay a final visit to the peak of Puy Mary as this volcanic pyramid dominates the local landscape and from it many of the features that link the underlying structures to the form of the land can be interpreted.

Investigations of scenery are often hampered by problems of scale and of perspective, but an unusually clear appreciation of the landscape assemblages of the volcanic province of the Massif can be obtained from the summit of the Puy de Dôme which, at nearly 1500 metres, stands some 200 metres above the neighbouring heights. The view to the north (Plate 11) shows a fine alignment of conical hills and domes, while to the south this pattern, although present, is rather less clearly seen due to the obscuring effect of woodland. The Monts Dore are visible to the south-west, and on a clear day you can see the Cantal upland far to the south. Towards the west is extensive plateau country, cut by valleys such as that of the River Sioule, while eastwards this surface drops abruptly to the plain of Limagne, above which stand several flat-topped plateaux. Occasionally, under exceptional conditions, Mont Blanc can be seen 300 kilometres to the east.

The broad framework of this landscape was roughed out during the Tertiary. During early Oligocene times most of the area you can see was occupied by a planation surface, of which the plateau to the west is a fragment. This was disrupted by the Alpine earth movements which brought about a major subsidence of the country to the east. The base of the Limagne graben sank, near Riom, to some 3000 metres below the surface of the Plateau des Dômes. At the close of the Oligocene volanic activity began and has continued intermittently ever since. As far as the landscape is concerned, some of the most important volcanic events occurred during the Quaternary. The present relatively high altitude of the ancient planation surface is a result of uplift during the Miocene.

Inspection of the country north of the Puy de Dôme will reveal many details of the way in which volcanic activity can affect scenery. A path to the north leads first to the Petit Puy de Dôme, which is seen to have a summit crater. Investigation of this depression shows that it is developed in blackened or reddened, rubbly scoria. The colour of this material reflects its history. A reddish colour indicates that the material was close to the centre of eruption, remained hot, and was oxidized. A black colour suggests a much cooler environment. Apart from indicating temperature conditions, colour is helpful for preliminary identification of the type of volcanic rock. Basaltic material often appears black to grey, while more acid lavas, trachytes, may appear pearly grey, beige, or nearly white.

Further north the path crosses the Traversin plateau, whose soil is made up of fragments of grey and black lava, red and black volcanic ash, and bedrock. After about 400 metres the track enters a valley, or atrio, whose eastern wall is a flank of the recent volcanic cone of Pariou. The western slope of the atrio is the inner crater wall of an ancient cone. It is clear that the Puy de Pariou is a complicated feature, and the evidence suggests a first phase of cone construction (ancient Pariou), then an episode of further explosive activity when the present cone was built inside the old crater. The current cone has its own crater which is about 96 metres deep and 300 metres in diameter. Investigation of the northern side of Pariou will reveal a further complication. The rim of the older crater is breached, and a lava flow has followed the depression to the north.

The Puy de Pariou is a complicated example of more than sixty similar volcanic structures that extend over a north–south distance of some 30 kilometres. Most are scoria cones built of volcanic fragments, and their various types are illustrated in the diagrams (Fig. 44). The type of volcanic activity that produced them is called Strombolian, after Stromboli, a volcanic island lying north-east of Sicily. The explosive phase was moderate and rhythmic, with periodic lava emission, and built up the cones we see today. The simple cones, for example, Puy de Jumes and Puy des Goules, were probably built during a single eruptive episode, lasting up to several months. The outer slope of each cone tends to be gently concave, reflecting the relatively steep angle at which the coarser fragments near the crater could stand, and the gentler angle at the margin of the cone associated with finer debris that was thrown further. In many cases erosion has reduced the angles of the outer slopes below their originally steeper gradients, so that maximum slopes are now about 30°. The steepest slope of an active Strombolian volcano is about 35°.

A striking variety of Strombolian volcano occurs when a sector of the original cone is missing. Such a form is called *égueulé*, or open-mouthed. It may result from a bias in the deposition of volcanic debris due perhaps to a constant wind direction, but a more likely explanation attributes the 'mouth' to the continuous excavation of scoria by a lava flow leaving the crater. The Puys of La Vache and Lassolas are fine examples of *égueulé* volcanoes.

From the summit of the Puy de Pariou the view south is dominated by the

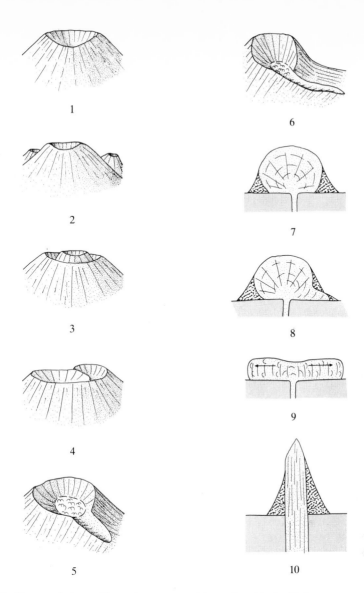

Fig. 44. The morphology of the various cones and domes found in the Chaîne:

(1) Normal symmetric cone with crater, for example Puy des Goules.

(2) Main cone, with parasitic cone development along radial weaknesses, for example Puy de la Nugère.

(3) Cone-within-cone arrangment, for example Puy de Côme (see also Fig. 42).

(4) Excentric cone-within-cone arrangement, for example Puy de Pariou.

(5) Partly open-mouthed cone, for example Puy de Louchadière.

(6) Completely open-mouthed cone, for example Puy de la Vache.

(7) Dome, resulting from the extrusion of viscous lava, for example Clierzou. Note the arrangement of fractures. One set is parallel to the surface, the other is at right angles.

(8) A combined dome and flow, resulting from lava extrusion over a sloping surface, for example Sarcoui.

(9) A dome-flow showing two directions of movement, for example Bois d'Aldit (Cantal).

(10) Needle-like form which was extruded vertically, for example the Sucs du Velay. The height of the needle is usually two to three times its diameter.

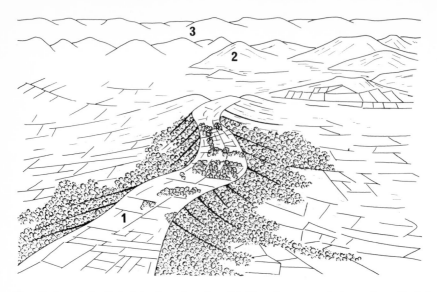

Fig. 45. Inverted relief of the Serre lava flow (1). Note the contrast between the cultivated surface of the flow and its wooded slopes. The buttes of Limagne (2) dominate the plain in the middle distance and the Forez hills (3) make up the background.

imposing Puy de Dôme, whose northern slope is particularly well displayed. Although this Puy is within the north–south trending band of cone-like forms its origin was quite different, and can be understood by reference to various aspects of its shape. The western portion is made up of a flat summit and steep slopes, characterized by narrow radial ridges that are separated by ravines. The appearance is consistent with cumulo-dome development, the extrusion of highly viscous lava that was unable to flow far from its vent. This type of volcanic activity is called Peléan, after Mont Pelée in Martinique. The radial ridges are original features, linked to lateral expansion, and not the result of erosion. The general impression is one of freshness, supported by the presence of many original needle-like features, and this view is confirmed by the date for the formation of the cumulo-dome, which is 6350 BC. The eastern portion of the Puy appears quite different. It has a conical form, with the summit constituting the highest point of the Puy, and is built of fragmental volcanic materials. This unit was formed as a result of explosive activity which breached the eastern side of the cumulo-dome. Only about eight similar dome-like forms are found in the Chaîne des Puys, including Le Petit Suchet and Sarcoui, which can be seen by looking north from the Puy de Dôme.

These volcanic cones and domes are perhaps the most striking feature of the Chaîne des Puys, but the more modest lava flows offer many points of interest. They generally stand at the base of a cone, as indeed does the eastern flow of the Puy de Pariou, and then continue in ribbon-like form for as much as 20 kilometres. The flows in the vicinity of Pariou are well worth investigating. From the Col des Goules, just north of the Puy, the road (N141) runs south-east towards Clermont-Ferrand. It soon crosses the flow we examined in the 'atrio' and its highly irregular, almost chaotic surface, locally called *cheire*, can be inspected. Such a surface form, referred to as *aa* by vulcanologists, results from the dislocation of a rapidly congealing lava skin as still molten lava flows beneath it. Just north of the road the lava has been quarried, and this exploitation of volcanic materials is common throughout the Chaîne.

A range of additional scenic details, developed on lava flows, can be investigated elsewhere in the Auvergne. On some flows, for example those between the Puys of Beaunit and Verrières, escaping gas has raised a series of blisters. The Cheire of Aydat shows tumuli, or small domes upwarped by the pressure of flowing lava. Tunnels occurred in some flows and when their roofs collapsed small linear ridges remained. This is the origin of the ribs of the Aydat *cheire*. A final feature to note is the development of pressure ridges, a result of congealing lava buckling under stress from above, and which are finely developed at Les Giullaumes, below the Puys de Barme.

The flows that we have examined so far were active relatively recently and so the valleys they occupied have shown little change. The older flows, extruded several million years ago, also occupied the major valleys of the time, but the action of various agents of erosion has drastically changed their position in the landscape (Fig. 45). From a vantage point on the road that climbs steeply from Volvic to Chateau Tournoël one has a fine view to the east and can see the nature of the changes than have occurred. The flat-topped Lachaud plateau can be seen towards the south-east, and a closer inspection will reveal that this is capped by a lava flow. It is reasonable to suppose that the lava occupied the low ground of the time, and that its present height is a result of the erosion of adjacent soft rocks. This plateau provides an excellent illustration of a variety of inverted relief, and its general arrangement is repeated in a series of flat-topped ridges that trend from west to east and extend like promontories into the Limagne Trough (Fig. 40). Another kind of inversion is shown in Fig. 46.

The Plateau de Gergovie, south of Clermont-Ferrand, is another fine example of inverted relief. It is capped by a Miocene basalt that gives rise to a flat summit surface, abruptly terminated by cliffs or steep slopes. The panorama from the summit includes many of the important land-forms of the area. The plateau of the Côtes de Clermont, surmounted by Miocene lava flows, can be seen to the north, while to the west you can identify the fault escarpment of Limagne, the Chaîne des Puys, and Mont Dore. The inverted relief of the Montagne de la Serre (Fig. 45), capped by a Pliocene lava flow, is visible to the south.

While ash cones and lava flows provide good illustrations of constructional land-forms, vulcanicity may also be associated with destructive action which

107

Fig. 46. Oligocene limestones capped by old river gravels of the Allier near Dallet about 10 kilometres east of Clermont-Ferrand. The height of the gravels, together with the presence of lava pebbles, suggest that the Allier has achieved considerable erosion since the volcanic episode.

can create its own distinctive relief. Drive about 4 kilometres west of Besse en Chandesse, along N678, and a short diversion leads to the impressive Lac Pavin, surrounded by coniferous woodland. An important clue towards the origin of this lake is provided by its shape, which is close to a circle some 750 metres in diameter. Such a shape could hardly be achieved by the damming of a river valley, and it is believed that Lac Pavin occupies a crater formed by a major volcanic explosion, perhaps caused by percolating ground water coming into contact with molten lava at depth. Part of the debris of the explosion fell around the rim of the crater, and locally buried the soil of the time. This ancient soil, or palaeosol, has been dated by the radiocarbon technique as 3450 years old. It is possible that the Pavin explosion was witnessed by early man. This type of explosive crater is called a *maar*, after the type examples found in the Eifel district of Western Germany. In the Chaîne des Puys several such *maars* have been investigated, including the Gour de Tazenat, the maar de Beaunit, and the smaller craters of Espinasse and Ampoix.

Volcanic activity is generally associated with the emission of large quantities of water vapour which may lead to heavy rainfall, and it is clear that the combination of water and ash could, at least in theory, give rise to extensive debris flows. Evidence is available near Perrier, about 4 kilometres west of Issoire on N496, that this situation may have occurred. Follow a steep footpath up the northern side of the valley and you will arrive at a cliff into which man has carved a number of cave-dwellings, or grottes. The rock is clearly soft, and close inspection shows it to consist of unsorted angular volcanic blocks, of variable size, set in a fine, ashy matrix. It is believed that this material was explosively ejected by a volcano in the region of Mont Dore. At the base of the deposit layers of partly rounded, coarse sands and gravels can be examined. The volcanic debris is evidence that a thick mud flow, or lahar, lubricated by heavy rainfall, swept down the valley of the time and buried already existing river gravels. It has been possible to date this event by an investigation of fossils found in the river gravels. These include the remains of varieties of rhinoceros, deer, and sabre-toothed tiger, which lived about two million years ago, thus suggesting that the lahar occurred just before the start of the Quaternary.

So far we have been investigating the immediate effect of volcanic activity, such as recent cones, flows, and explosive craters, and the results of a lengthy period of erosion, for example the inverted relief of the Limagne plateaux. Between these two extremes lies a group of land-forms whose character results from a partial destruction of volcanic rocks. A journey along the N496 from Champeix to Lac Chambon will provide illustrations of this theme. The road follows the incised valley of the Couze de Chambon, the floor of which is occupied by the basaltic Tartaret flow. This is one of the longest flows in the Auvergne, extending for 22 kilometres between Neschers and Murol. This flow shows a typically rugged *cheire* appearance, but the degree to which it has been dissected by the present river should be noted. Locally, the Couze has cut a gorge-like river valley, some 15 metres deep, whose floor has so far failed to penetrate the base of the flow. The relatively fresh, unweathered lava of the gorge walls contrasts strikingly with the upper clinkery horizon that has been occasionally dissected into pinnacles, while the steep slopes of the original valley climb away from the lava. This scenery is typical of the zones where the Couze has carved its valley through granitic horsts. When grabens filled with relatively soft sediment crop out, for example just east of Montaigut le Blanc, the valley widens and the scenery becomes more muted. These results of erosion contrast with constructive features that can be seen just east of Murol, where many miniature volcanoes, 5–30 metres high, were forced up by steam as the fresh lava flowed over a marshy valley floor.

The partial dissection of a lava flow by stream activity, together with evidence of pre-lava conditions, can be readily investigated in the valley of the River Rhue (Fig. 47), just north-east of the tourist centre of Égliseneuve

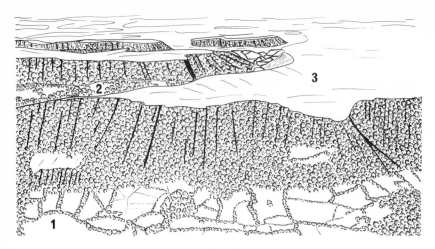

Fig. 47. View across the *planèze* of Limon (3) which slopes from 1500 metres to 1300 metres on the northern slopes of the Cantal. The valley of the Santoire (1) is in the foreground, and that of the Rhue (2) in the middle distance.

d'Entraigues. A short walk along N678 from the village takes you to a waterfall on the right-hand side of the road (Fig. 48). Examination will reveal that the Rhue is falling over the edge of a lava flow that is confined within a larger valley, and that its downstream section is cut well below the base of the lava. Now examine the base of the flow beside the waterfall, and you will find small, rounded pebbles. The evidence suggests that the lava occupied a valley whose floor, veneered by river gravels, lay above the level of the present stream. The flow was subsequently dissected by the Rhue which has extended headwards to the present position of the waterfall. This situation is very similar to that described for the Castellfullit area in Catalonia.

The interplay between volcanic rock and other surface processes is well displayed west of Murol, where the main valley is blocked by the fine Strombolian cone of Tartaret, the source of the lava flow that occupies the Couze de Chambon. There is, however, evidence to suggest that another process has also been at work. From the eastern end of Lake Chambon an amphitheatre-shaped land-form with near vertical sides can be seen away to the north. This feature, the Saut de la Pucelle, may have originated as an explosive crater or as a result of collapse, but its present significance is that it is the site of a major landslide which flowed south and assisted in the damming of Lake Chambon. The lake itself is only about a quarter of its original size, as it is being steadily silted up by debris carried by the Couze and by material washed from the adjacent hill-slopes. This theme of lake formation through the damming effect of volcanic activity is quite common in the Auvergne and you can see a further example about 20 kilometres south-west of Clermont-Ferrand, where the River Veyre has been dammed

Fig. 48. Waterfall at Égliseneuve-d'Entraigues. The River Rhue has cut through a lava flow which occupies an ancient valley. Water-rounded gravel may be found at the base of the lava.

by the Cheire d'Aydat, flowing from the Puy de Lassolas and the Puy de la Vache. The result is the Lac d'Aydat, comparable in size to Chambon.

Inspection of the Chaudefour valley, which is the natural continuation of the valley containing Lake Chambon, should convince you that a further agent or erosion has been at work in the higher region of the Auvergne. The upper valley is U-shaped, is mantled by slumped debris, and terminates in a fine cirque beyond which rise the jagged summits of the Puy de Sancy. This evidence suggests the work of former glaciers, an impression that is re-inforced by a drive along D36 around the head of Chaudefour and towards Le Mont Dore. The road passes the village of Monaux, set on the flat floor of a glaciated valley that hangs abruptly over the northern slopes of the Chaudefour trough. The tributary glacier that occupied the Monaux valley was unable to keep pace with the rapid downcutting of the main Chaudefour ice tongue, and a classic example of a hanging valley has resulted. The journey to Le Mont Dore will provide fine panoramic views of a glaciated environment.

It is well worth driving south of the town along N483 and up the glacial trough of the Upper Dordogne to the foot of the Puy de Sancy. Here, in season, one can travel by cable-car to the summit of the Puy and examine the details of this spectacular landscape. Perhaps the most immediately dramatic sight is provided by many sheer pinnacles that can be seen during the ascent. They are a result of frost shattering, which selectively attacked the rocks of the Puy at a time when the valleys below were occupied by glaciers.

The long, even skyline of the eastern wall of the Upper Dordogne trough provides a piece of evidence that draws attention to the development of the landscape on the larger scale. To understand its significance, it should be appreciated that the Mont Dore region is the dissected remnant of a huge complex volcano that originally covered some 800 square kilometres. It was built as a result of contrasting episodes of explosive cinder emission, basaltic lava flow, and intrusive activity (the pinnacles that can be seen on the ascent to the summit are made of the intrusive rock locally called Sancyite). Many millions of years were required for the production of this stratovolcano, and activity seems to have finally ceased during the Ice Age. The structure was then deeply eroded by valley glaciers, but the long, even skyline is a surviving fragment of an extensive basaltic sheet that flowed down the slopes of the ancient volcano (see Fig. 47).

The volcanic region of the Auvergne offers the investigator a great variety of land-forms, varying from simple cones, flows, and explosive craters through increasingly complicated landscapes that result from the action of different agents of erosion over varying periods of time. Each event left behind one or more clues that contribute towards the unravelling of land-form history.

A striking aspect of the scenery of the Chaîne des Puys and Mont Dore is the chaotic yet constant association of forest, scrub, rough grazing, and fields. The visual pattern is further complicated by the steady replacement of traditional land-use practices with entirely new ones. Nowhere is this more evident than in the mixed character of the forest. The extensive seminatural stands of beech were once an integral part of the rural economy, but are not now systematically exploited for fuel and timber. Their former unity has been progressively disrupted, since about 1860 by coniferous afforestation (Plate 12) in numerous small, and several large, blocks. Similarly, much of the communally owned rough grazing has been abandoned to scrub encroachment or has subsequently been afforested. Indeed, many fields have also shared the same fate. Conversely, in some districts the chequer-board array of small fields, broadleaved woods, small plantations, and pasture has been reorganized to produce larger parcels of land for agriculture and forestry, as part of a planned programme of rural improvement. In essence, then, we are confronted with a landscape in transition, embracing several elements of continuity and change. The old way of life has broken down and a rather different one is emerging.

In the early part of the last century three types of farming prevailed in the area. Sheep-rearing for wool and meat generally prevailed, with flocks being grazed on common pastures, or *landes*. This emphasis on livestock as opposed to arable crops reflects the impoverished soils associated with the granitic *socle*, the widespread acidic lavas, and the wet climate. On the steeper volcanic slopes, incidentally, intense grazing often encouraged soil erosion, to the extent that expanses of the underlying ash and cinders were exposed. Good examples of this can still be seen on the flanks of several puys, including, going from south to north: Combgrasse, L'Enfer, la Vache, Lassolas, and Pariou. Typically the *landes* were some distance from the village. For instance the *landes* of Suchet and Pariou have been grazed, right up to the present, by flocks from the villages of Les Fontêtes, les Roches, and la Fontaine du Berger. Arable fields were concentrated nearer to the village, and produced a range of subsistence crops, principally rye. Such fields are particularly extensive around the villages of Beaune and Laschamp. The tradition of *morcellement*, where a farmer's holding was subdivided after his death amongst his heirs, with each having a balance of different soil types, led to the creation of very small fields, averaging 30–40 ares in extent (1 are = 100 square metres). In one case near la Croix, 125 hectares (1 hectare = 10 000 square metres) were subdivided into 162 parcels, which were collectively grazed and subsequently abandoned. The field boundaries were often walled with blocks of dark lava or planted with trees like ash, elm, and beech. Ash is a strong, supple wood ideal for tool handles, while the wood of elm does not readily split and was thus used for the rims of waggon wheels. Beech provided, and continues to provide, firewood in winter, whereas in summer, foliage was lopped off it to provide supplementary feed for cattle. Finally, crops were also produced on temporary plots scattered over the *landes*. These plots were cleared by burning and were then cultivated for a short while until their fertility declined.

Apart from the *landes* and fields, large tracts of beechwoods were also owned. Again, these were often sectioned into individual holdings. Some of the holdings on the volcanic cones took the form of very narrow strips aligned towards the summits of the cones. Today these are conspicuous as strips of beech of different girth and height on the flanks of Puy de Côme and Puy de Louchadière. On the former there were 185 such strips, each 500–600 metres long and just a few metres wide. The beechwoods supplied timber for fuel, carpentry, clogs, skis, plough yokes, and smaller farm implements. Other common tree species in the woods are: whitebeam, which is most common on the higher ground; sweet chestnut, the fruits of which, in some parts of the Massif Central, were once ground into flour during times of hardship; and field maple, whose wood, like that of ash, was much prized for tool handles. Beneath the woodland canopy, there is sometimes an underwood of hazel, which was periodically cut for sticks. Characteristically, the broadleaved woodlands are found on steep slopes that were unsuited to grazing or ploughing. This explains their concentration in the valleys incised into the edge of the basement complex, opening out into Limagne. A second concentration occurs on the puys and in the valleys dissecting Mont Dore. Usually they are most widely developed on shaded, north-facing slopes.

On Mont Dore, harsh winters with prolonged snow-cover ensured that the high pastures, or *montagnes*, above the trees could only be used seasonally. Stockmen went up with their herds of cattle in early summer and lived in stone-built shelters or *burons*. The milk was converted into the famous *fromages bleus* of Auvergne. This second type of farming, based on transhumance, or the seasonal movement of stock and people, has essentially disappeared in its traditional form.

The third and last farming type of the early 1800s was vine growing. It was restricted to the sunnier slopes overlooking the lowlands around Clermont-Ferrand and Riom. The vineyards were normally very small and often terraced into the hillsides. With the exception of those around Chateaugay, they have been abandoned, although their outlines are still clearly evident from the N9.

The decline of these various agrarian activities began in the 1840s. Poor harvests, the weakening of craft industries in the face of competition from factory-produced goods, improved communications (including new road and rail links) and the subsequent importation of cheaper foods, were all contributory factors to an exodus of the rural population which was attracted to the growing urban centres off the plateau. Towards the end of the nineteenth century, moreover, the vineyards were devastated by the vine-root disease, *Phylloxera*, and this intensified the out-migration. The loss has continued throughout this century, so that the remaining agricultural community is relatively old and much reduced. However it is still larger than the French national average.

Hence, the more remote *landes*, especially those with complex ownership patterns, have been progressively abandoned, along with many fields. Abandoned fields are most obvious, perhaps, on the chaotic lava surfaces of the *cheires*. Free of grazing or cultivation, these abandoned areas have been invaded by broom and, to lesser extent, by heather and bracken. Colonization by these plants is soon followed by the establishment of a scrub or thicket, chiefly of birch, though hazel, blackthorn, or willow may be present as well.

Significant deliberate changes in the landscape also commenced in the nineteenth century, as the first conifer plantations were laid out. Earlier phases of woodland clearance for pasture in the mountains of the Massif Central were thought to have been the indirect cause of catastrophic floodings in the Rhône and Loire valleys, and so gave rise to a law on upland afforestation in 1860. The forest which covers Puy de Charmont was created by an application of this law in 1886. In fact as early as 1827 the Prefect of the Puy de Dôme administrative region had consulted the Count of Montlosier on ways of converting sterile hill-land back to forest. Experimental plantings were made around his chateau at the foot of Puy de Montchal and his descendants have established several plantations in the same area. The initial stages of coniferous afforestation generated much conflict between foresters and farmers. Plantations limited the run of flocks and herds, while the farmers themselves could not afford to plant, because the revenue from timber is long deferred.

Since 1900 the area under forest has more than doubled, and doubtless much of the abandoned land will also be planted with trees. Unfortunately much of the planting was done in an uncoordinated manner, which has exacerbated the long-standing enmity between pastoralism and forestry. Absentee landlords unwilling to lease small plots of land to neighbouring farmers planted them instead, a development which has been referred to as postage-stamp afforestation. This caused problems of shade, pest invasion, and disruption of drainage in the adjacent fields and pasture. After 1945 much of the afforestation was achieved through the *Fonds Forestier National*. Government agencies are unable to plant areas of less than 25 hectares but there is no such restriction on private landowners who account for the great majority of the existing woodland. Grants have been made available for small plots and much of the postage-stamp afforestation was actually financed in this way. In fact, the average size of plantations that have been financed by grants in the Massif Central as a whole is only 1.5 hectares.

Larger projects are funded through favourable loans or contracts. Thus a village may undertake re-afforestation of a block of land, and though an individual may have sole use of a section, the land belongs to the village, and the section is tied to the house. In other words, the block of land is a territorial collective, worked individually. This is a modern form of an archaic regional practice and of the 100 000 hectares of public forest in Auvergne, about 60 000 belong to 1700 sections. There are many instances of plantations owned by villages. Those on Puy de L'Enfer and Puy de la Rodde are fairly recent and belong to Espinasse and la Garandie, respectively. Those on the Puy de Salomon and Puy de Grosmanaux were originally planted at the end of the last century, and belong to the neighbouring villages of Allagnat, Laschamp, and Manson. Some of the communal holdings are very large, with the two most important communes – Nebouzat and Saint-Genes-Champanelle – having 5200 hectares between them.

Apart from the native silver fir, a wide range of species has been planted, including the common spruce, Scots pine, Austrian pine, larch, and some Douglas fir. Pine, larch, and oak demand light in contrast to the silver fir and beech which can endure shade. Spruce has intermediate requirements in this respect. Some of the foresters of the last century used a judicious mix of pine, spruce, fir, and broadleaved hardwoods. Pine was included because it relieved the shade by admitting more light into the plantation. Spruce was employed to fill gaps in the immature plantation, before the supply of timber was assured. Eventually both species were eliminated leaving the dark firs, which were able to regenerate naturally beneath the mother trees and so perpetuate the plantation. The broadleaved hardwoods were incorporated to help maintain the soil fertility. This tradition of natural regeneration is still followed in many of the plantations; although it makes for difficult exploitation of the mature timber, it avoids the visual scars associated with clear-felling, not to mention the formal regularity of planting lines. One further point is that there is a tendency to favour spruce on the wetter west-facing slopes, and pine on the drier east-facing slopes. The contrast between the dark spruce and the lighter-coloured pines is especially pronounced around Mont Dore.

The types of land ownership, the various assortments of hardwoods and conifers, and different management practices (some dating from medieval times), have resulted in a diverse forest scene. There is far less of the monotony which is commonly associated with commercial afforestation in, say, the uplands of Britain. The autumn symphony of colour on the hillsides emphasizes this point. The rich gilt of the birch and larch, the incandescent tints of the beech and the silvery hues of the whitebeam, all contrast with the flecks, patches, and blocks of mainly evergreen conifers. Even with the latter there is some diversity, ranging from the sombre firs to the blue–green foliage of the pines with their pinkish-brown trunks. Regrettably this scene will change, for the beechwoods, which make up roughly half of the total wooded area, have little economic value now. Many are likely to be clear-felled and replanted with conifers.

Changes in the pattern of the cultivated land have proceeded alongside the developments in afforestation. Land parcels have been exchanged and regrouped to obtain a more rational arrangement, and thereafter zoned, as appropriate, for arable cultivation, pasture, and forestry. Where this has been achieved, the traditional tension between the farmer and forester has been greatly eased. The cost of reorganizing the old patchwork of land parcels is considerable, and progress has therefore been slow. Hedges and conifer spinneys have to be grubbed up, walls removed, and a new farming infrastructure provided. The natural conservatism of many of the older farmers has acted as a further check.

Very recently, allied changes have been initiated in some of the *montagnes* of the Massif Central. After 1945, it became very difficult to find stockmen to accompany herds on to the mountaintops in summer and to live in the *burons*, and by the 1950s the seasonal migration had practically ceased. The result was that the pastures deteriorated, as heather, myrtle, and broom invaded. A solution to the problem was devised in Cantal, immediately south of Mont Dore, and entailed a form of ranching. The *montagnes* were rearranged into 200-hectare units, and further subdivided into five or six sections for purposes of rotational grazing. Individually owned herds were then grouped together and sent up to the newly improved pastures with a few expert stockmen. Such cooperative ventures are now being extended into adjacent areas.

The only entirely new land-use activity to affect the Chaînes des Puys and Mont Dore is recreation. Winter sports have been developed at Mont Dore, as the ski-lifts and new holiday accommodation demonstrate. However, both areas are very popular with tourists in the summer months, and a growing number of old and new houses are serving as second homes. To help reconcile the various competing land uses, a regional park – the Parc des Volcans – was set up. Its aims are to preserve the amenity value of the landscape, the harmonious development of forestry and agriculture, and to safeguard the flora and fauna.

The visitor to the Chaîne des Puys is continually struck by the importance of recent geological events as he examines volcanoes and lava flows that have been little altered since their construction. This theme of recency is the dominant motif within both the restricted area of the Chaîne and the larger northern volcanic province of the Massif. Volcanicity began at the close of Oligocene times and has continued intermittently ever since, associated with major fractures in the basement rocks. The last event occurred about 1000 AD. There are few regions within Europe where the land-forms show such a simple and direct response to geological events.

There are, however, many examples in the Auvergne of land-forms that owe their present shape to erosional processes. The *planèzes* of Mont Dore and the inverted relief of the lava flows that extend into the plain of Limagne are a response to geomorphological processes which were particularly active during the Quaternary.

The plant assemblages that clothe the volcanic slopes take up the theme of recency, for during the last 150 years there have been major changes in land use and consequently of vegetational patterns. The unity of the old beech woods is now broken by extensive conifer plantations, and the former intricate pattern of small field, woods, and pastures is being reorganized into large economic units. Thus, the processes that fashioned the present landscape have occurred remarkably recently when considered in the perspective of geological and human time-scales.

6 Catalonia

Catalonia is one of the major tourist centres of Europe, and both its coastline and hinterland are renowned for their beauty. Unknown to the majority of visitors, it is also a unique geological region, for it represents the collision zone between mainland Europe and the Iberian 'subcontinent'. It is bounded to the north by the Pyrenees and to the south-east by the coastal mountains of the Catalanides. Between these two mountainous regions is the lowland area of the Ebro depression and, as you will see, this is an area characterized by the presence of Mesozoic and Cainozoic rocks.

Geologically the history of the region is complex with the rocks of the axial zone of the Pyrenees and of the Catalanides constituting the main outcrop of the Hercynian basement. In the axis of the Pyrenees the effects of the Hercynian Orogeny are dated around mid-Silurian and the sediments subjected to metamorphism are thus known to be lower Palaeozoic or earlier. The Pyrenees can be divided into several parallel east–west trending zones with strata of Mesozoic and Cainozoic age occurring in the outer zones on both the French and Spanish flanks. In the axial zone much of the higher ground is marked by the presence of granitic and gneissose masses emplaced during the major phases of mountain building.

In post-Hercynian times sediments of the Upper Palaeozoic and Mesozoic were deposited around the axial region. These deposits mark the erosion and destruction of the new chain. In the Lower Cretaceous a further phase of mountain building heralded a sequence of events which led to the reactivation of ancient fractures and the folding and metamorphism of the younger sediments. In the Cainozoic a major phase of compression resulted in the folding and faulting of the Upper Cretaceous and Cainozoic mantle.

In the Catalanides the story of the basement is rather similar to that of the Pyrenees, the high ground of the coast corresponding in the main to the granitic massif of the Costa Brava. Like the Pyrenees the Catalanides exerted a positive influence on sedimentation during the Mesozoic and Cainozoic eras. Palaeozoic rocks of the Catalanides are well exposed around Bagur and in the Sierras de las Gabarras, del Montseny and the Vall-Llobregat. To the west of the Ampurdan basin the high ground of the Sierra de Finestras consists of Hercynian basement rocks capped by nummulitic limestones of the Eocene.

In the cultural sense the region of Catalonia begins over the border in France, and the journey from Perpignan to Gerona will take you across the axial zone of the eastern Pyrenees. The initial part of the journey is across the alluvial plain of the Tet and Tech rivers, the continuity of which is broken only by the low-lying Pliocene outcrops around Perpignan and Banyuls-des-Aspres. On a clear day the sight of the Pyrenees is quite breath-taking and looking southwards from Banyuls or La Boulou one can see that the sharp break between plain and mountains is structurally controlled. Just south of La Boulou, the road to Perthus starts to climb steeply, with resistant Cambrian sediments and Palaeozoic mica schists forming the initial mountain slopes. Approximately half-way to Le Perthus the Cambrian deposits are faulted against rocks of the rugged Junquera Massif. Petrographically the Junquera 'granite' is variable in both grain size and mineralogy and in some localities the presence of certain plagioclase feldspars, biotite, or hornblende warrants the use of the term granodiorite. Elsewhere the rock may be noticeably coarse-grained with both alkali and plagioclase feldspars and subsidiary hornblende or biotite. In this case the rock is termed a 'monzonite'. The granite of the Junquera Massif is well exposed near the frontier town of the same name and some time should be spent in this region studying the relationships between the host rock and the younger veins and dykes that criss-cross exposed surfaces.

One kilometre east of La Junquera, on the road to Cantallops, a small quarry on the northern side of the road is of considerable interest. The quarry is cut so as to provide several accessible levels, and this permits a detailed study of numerous faces. In hand-specimen it can be seen that there are two different rock types present. The first of these is very fine-grained, grey–green in colour and with a laminated or platy texture. When rubbed between the fingers it has a soapy feel and when scratched it produces a powdery, talc-like residue. The rock is essentially a mica schist and its texture is markedly different from that of the second type. This has a granular texture with large grains of quartz set in a matrix of mica. Like the first it has a distinct, though less well-defined, lamination and it would be correct to assume that both rock types have undergone some degree of deformation, for these rocks are the products of the mechanical process of shearing and granulation, and are aptly termed cataclasites. In fact, they are the products of dislocation metamorphism on a grand scale; the products bearing little or no resemblance to the parent granitic rocks.

The shearing of the country rocks around La Junquera is linked with a major north-west to south-east trending fault, which extends from Figueras in the south to Le Perthus in the north. The granite and the previously noted Cambrian sediments are part of the Hercynian basement and were elevated into the axial zone of the Pyrenees during the Alpine Orogeny. Elevation preceded faulting. In the Pyrenees, Alpine metamorphism is usually rather weak and only Hercynian metamorphism, linked with the intrusion of the granites, is readily identifiable.

There are excellent sections across the metamorphosed Palaeozoic rocks of the eastern Pyrenees on the Cabo de Creuz peninsula west of La Junquera.

The best sections occur along the rugged coastline between Puerto de la Selva and Cap Gros, and north of Cadaques (Fig. 49) to the tip of Cabo de Creuz. As these sections extend for several kilometres it is wise to devote a whole day to a particular traverse and be equipped to tackle narrow coastal paths and difficult countryside. The Puerto de la Selva traverse begins to the east of the harbour. At first an unsurfaced road runs parallel to the coast and excellent exposures of slightly metamorphosed sandstones, psammites, are seen to exhibit second phase folding. The road extends eastwards as far as the first major bay and *en route* the sandstones are succeeded by finer-grained rocks that exhibit a well-defined cleavage. These argillaceous (clay-silt grade) rocks are termed 'pelites' and looking eastward one can see that they are cut by numerous discordant bodies. These are dykes and a close examination of any of the numerous exposed surfaces, will reveal that the constituent rock type is coarse-grained. It is composed mainly of quartz and alkali feldspars with micas and tourmaline as accessory minerals. Rocks of this type are termed pegmatites and the dyke swarms of Cabo de Creuz (Fig. 50) are probably associated with the granites emplaced at the end of the Carboniferous. The dykes are frequently fractured and folded and it is easy to judge the stage at which this actually took place.

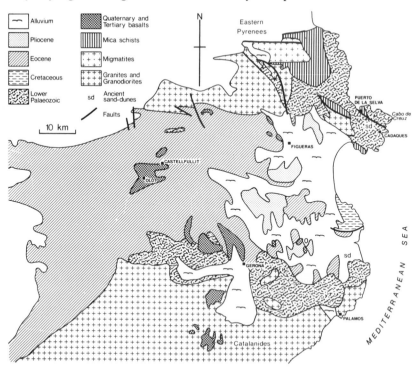

Fig. 49. The geology of the Ampurdan Basin, the Eastern Pyrenees, and the northern Catalanides.

Beyond the first bay the traverse becomes more difficult owing to an overall deterioration of the tracks. The difficulty of the route is however, matched by the splendour of the scenery and the complexity of the geology. Almost unbroken exposure reveals that the country rocks, the pelites, become increasingly more deformed with beautiful small-scale structures visible on numerous polished surfaces. Larger-scale shears, folds, and faults can also be observed and seemingly large and larger crystals can be collected from the pegmatites. At Cap Gros (Fig. 51) the long traverse is rewarded with a most spectacular view of a zone of mylonitization, where the pelites are generally streaked outwards and the pegmatites pinched into large eye-shaped structures termed augens. Garnets, cordierite, and andalusite are among the common minerals of this zone.

The traverse from Puerto de la Selva to Cap Gros crosses three zones of metamorphism and just to the east of the town the psammites form the core of a large synform. To confirm the presence of this structure it would be

Fig. 50. Resistant, coarse-grained pegmatite dyke striking approximately north–south across Cap Gros/Cabo de Creuz, north-east Catalonia. Numerous dykes are present and many are folded. The country rocks are mostly schists and phyllites.

121

necessary to plot the dip and strike measurements of both bedding and cleavage.

The rugged hills of the Cabo de Creuz stand high above the southerly flood plain of the River Fluvia. The flood plain is part of the Ampurdan Basin and this corresponds to the eastern extension of the Ebro Depression. In the coastal region, north of the Fluvia, the extensive cover of river gravels and sands is broken only by the occasional outcrop of Mesozoic limestones or Neogene volcanics. To the south of the Fluvia however, the scenery is much more varied, with the Montgri Massif dominating the coastline between Ampurias and Estartit. The Massif is composed essentially of Cretaceous limestones which, in the immediate vicinity of L'Escala, are characterized by numerous reef knolls. Between Ampurias and L'Escala the limestones are extensively potholed and in some holes fossil soils are covered by drapes of basaltic lava. Such detailed discoveries indicate that the limestones of the Montgri Massif were exposed long before the outpourings of the Neogene lavas. The latter are now confined to the western and southern regions of the Ampurdan depression and it is apparent that they once covered a much greater area than they do at the present time.

The regional dip of the Montgri limestone is to the north-west and the traveller from L'Escala to Estartit via Torroella de Montgri, will notice that the highest points of the Massif coincide with the southern scarp. The whole of the Montgri Massif is a thrust allochthonous block and evidence to prove this is obtainable to the west of the harbour at Estartit. There, a short distance beyond the sea-front villas, the Cretaceous limestones form towering cliffs. Access to the cliffs is difficult but even the most limited foray over the boulder-strewn beach will reveal that the blocks are mostly shattered and brecciated. The breccias are bound by a secondary calcite cement and the whole outcrop exhibits the effect of intense brittle fracture. The limestones rest on highly disturbed gypum-rich shales of Triassic age. Back towards the villas these shales are seen to rest upon compact, undisturbed red and yellow sandstones, grits, and conglomerates. Occasionally fossiliferous pebbles can be found that contain nummulites and therefore the rocks can be dated as Middle to Upper Tertiary. The succession at Estartit is therefore Tertiaries – Triassic and Cretaceous and this indicates that the last two have been thrust over the younger strata. In fact the Mesozoic block is thought to have been pushed many kilometres from a point of origin close to the Franco-Spanish border. The evidence from Estartit throws light on the development of this piece of coastline which is discussed in the section on land-forms.

To the south of Estartit from Playa de Pals to Sa Riera the Palaeozoic rocks of the Hercynian basement are extensively exposed. As at Puerto de la Selva the main rock type is a pelite and dykes, faults, and shear zones are again part of the basement story. At several localities beyond the promontory south of Playa de Pals and in and around the bay of Sa Riera, the

Palaeozoics are covered by conglomerates and breccias of Eocene age (Plate 13). Just north of the promontory in a small embayment the exposed breccias are very immature and the large angular blocks measure up to 2 metres across. Most are from the underlying basement and the field boundary is a marked angular unconformity. *En route* to Sa Riera the breccias are replaced laterally by well-rounded (mature), but coarse-grained, conglomerates. These rocks are well sorted and on several fresh surfaces pebbles of pelites, granites, and Mesozoic limestones are easily recognized. Note also that many pebbles are interlocked as a result of pressure solution. This phenomenon takes place when some rocks actually become like a plastic or even a viscous fluid owing to the great weight of overlying materials.

Between Playa de Pals and Sa Riera the conglomerates are overlain by nummulitic limestones and these thin westwards toward an ancient shoreline. Algal and coral reefs occur above the conglomerates on the south side of the Bay of Sa Riera, and these in turn are overlain by thin nummulitic limestones and contorted ferruginous sandstones. At first this sequence may be somewhat confusing, but a careful collection of data will suggest that the disturbed nature of these sediments is due to downslope slumping. This phenomenon may possibly be linked with local crustal disturbance.

Crustal disturbance in northern Catalonia was also responsible for the volcanic activity of the Olot and Selva districts. Around Olot the clues are obvious, with large scoriaceous cones and valley-guided lava flows that are discussed in the section on land-forms (p. 128). In the Selva region the

Fig. 51. Coastal outcrop approximately 3 kilometres to the south-east of Puerto de la Selva, northern Catalonia. The rocks occur in the highest metamorphic zone of the Cabo de Creuz. Note that the lighter coloured, igneous rocks have been pinched and stretched to form 'birds-eye', or augen, structures.

cones are lacking but well-jointed basaltic flows are very much in evidence. At Hostalrich a volcanic flow sits directly on the basement granite and is itself covered by a complex sequence of waterlain volcanoclastics.

Granites are very much in evidence in the southern region of northern Catalonia. Excellent exposures occur all along the coastline from just south of Bagur to Barcelona, and detailed investigations will yield a great deal of information on their composition and post-emplacement history. Fine-grained aplite and coarse-grained pegmatite dykes are common (Fig. 52) as are faults and shear zones. In many outcrops there is a circular banding on the surface of granite. The banding alternates in colour, which shows that this is a result of weathering. The circular structures are termed liesegang rings. Weathering is a pronounced feature of the Catalan granites, and inland many are rotted to a depth of several metres. In these areas the granite literally has a gritty texture.

No visit to Catalonia would be complete without seeing the seminary at Montserrat. *En route* it is advisable to stop and view not only the geology but also the general scenery. Approaching the Massif of Montserrat itself (Plate 14) you will be impressed by its size and grandeur, and will see that the red terrestrial sediments at the base contrast greatly with white materials that form the bulk of the Massif. These materials are massively bedded con-glomerates (Fig. 53) which were initially several thousand metres thick.

Fig. 52. Fine-grained, aplite veins cutting the granitic rocks of the Costa Brava. Granitic rocks crop out from Fornells north of Palamos to Badalona in the south. The composition of the granites varies considerably and their history is complex. Blocks of country rock may be found within the granite mass.

They represent the site of an ancient delta and mark the existence of this structure throughout much of the early Cainozoic era. An analysis of the clasts will show some comparison with those at Sa Riera and the phenomenon of pressure solution is immediately obvious. The rounded masses above the seminary (Plate 15) are, for many people, a unique experience in the field of geomorphology.

The attention of most of the summer visitors to Catalonia is undoubtedly focused on the coastal fringe and while this is scenically attractive, the inland regions also have much to offer. A convenient way of understanding their general arrangement is to seek out a good vantage point such as the medieval town of Pals (Fig. 54) 9 kilometres north of Palafrugell. The view to the north-east includes extensive flat country, the plains of Ampurdan, its patchwork appearance reflecting various types of cultivation. To the south-west the plain seems to lap abruptly against well-wooded high ground, culminating in the Sierra de las Gabarras at 531 metres. To the north, you may glimpse the Pyrenees. Pals itself rises like an island because it is built on a sandstone that is much more resistant than the adjacent soft sediments of the plain. The distant uplands are similarly resistant although both faulting and folding have made a contribution to their relative height. Faulting may also have led to volcanic activity, an important ingredient in the scenery around Olot, which lies far to the north-west.

Fig. 53. Close up of the conglomeratic deposits of Montserrat. Note that the rocks are of several different varieties and that pressure has resulted in a degree of plasticity. This is reflected in the irregular contact between various pebbles and the 'flow' of some shales and limestones around more resistant igneous and quartzitic rocks.

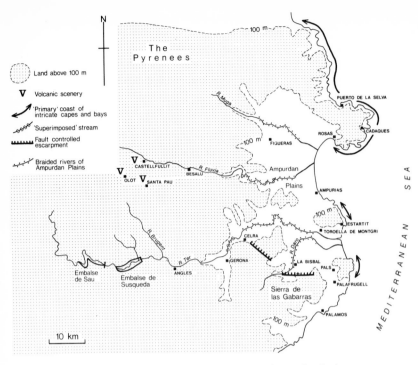

Fig. 54 Location map and main landscape features of north-east Catalonia.

The scenery is not, however, simply a response to various rock types and structures; surface processes, notably the work of rivers, have made a major contribution. Valuable pieces of evidence can be collected by studying almost any Catalonian river, but the course of the Ter provides an excellent example, and in addition provides many clues illuminating the history of the landscape as a whole.

A suitable starting-point is at the bridge over the Ter just south of Verges, 13 kilometres north of La Bisbal. The bridge itself provides the first clue. It is much wider than the present channel, and its southern section consists of a number of apparently unnecessary arches. In reality, however, these arches are designed as spillways to carry an excess of discharge, and so imply considerable variations in the volume of river flow. The river channel itself provides further pieces of evidence. It is braided in character (like so many Catalonian streams) and the pattern of vegetation on the bars may suggest the way in which they developed. The downstream tip of each bar appears to be the oldest part, as it supports well-grown willows, while the upstream section has only been colonized by grasses and herbs. This evidence may show that the bars have been built up by deposition in an upstream direction from an original nucleus around the site of the oldest vegetation.

Now examine the exposed edge of the river channel, which provides you

126

with a natural section through the sediments laid down by the stream. Notice first of all how the calibre of these river deposits changes from the base to the top of the section. The lowest exposed materials are quite coarse in nature, up to 25 centimetres in length, while the overlying sediments become steadily finer, culminating in a silty clay at the top. This sequence suggests that the sediments were deposited by a stream whose energy at this particular site was steadily diminishing. A natural question at this point concerns the width of these river deposits. Some scientists have suggested that much of the Ampurdan lowland is veneered by these deposits, and you can get some idea of their width by looking at the extent of gravel workings near the River Fluvia south of Torroella de Fluvia. A good range of rock types is represented in the Ter deposits, notably dark volcanic rocks, which have clearly originated far upstream and which, therefore, provide good evidence of a stream's ability to transport sediment.

The Ter is not only a good example of a braided stream, but its valley also provides evidence about earlier stages in the development of the scenery. Drive from Gerona on the main La Bisbal road, and about 3 kilometres west of Celra you will pass through a striking, steep-sided valley, the gorge of San Julian de Ramis, which is followed by road and rail, as well as by the Ter itself. This arrangement presents a major problem, which is to explain the circumstances under which the Ter could cut through the high ground near Celra, an extension of the Sierra de las Gabarras, on its way to the sea. Rock exposures that may clarify this problem are visible at several sites on the way to La Bisbal. A number of roadside cuttings show soft, reddish Tertiary sediments cropping out at a height well above their Ampurdan plains level. This suggests that the Tertiary rocks may once have been thick enough to have mantled the north-west extension of the Gabarras. The early Ter may have flowed across the surface of these rocks and, with the passage of time, cut down its valley in keeping with a lowering of the surface of the Ampurdan plains. It then met, and incised, the Lower Palaeozoic schists of the Gabarras spur. Further erosion culminated in the present valley form. This process, which gives rise to a valley whose course is inexplicable in terms of the present landscape, is called superimposition of drainage.

The Ter valley has further information to reveal, which can be investigated in its upper reaches, between Angles and the Susqueda reservoir. There is a fine viewpoint just downsteam of the reservoir dam, from which you can easily examine the attractive, bold simplicity of the valley. As you can see it is deeply incised and this, together with the sinuous course of the river, gives rise to a fine sequence of interlocking spurs. The profiles of these spurs show a rather abrupt steepening towards their bases, and this may suggest that the downcutting of the Ter accelerated appreciably during the final stages. The valley side slopes are straight and terminate upward in narrow, convex ridges, an arrangement which is believed to result from erosion chiefly by surface-water flow.

On the way down the valley towards the lower reservoir, occasional roadside cuttings reveal patches of well-rounded pebbles set in a sandy matrix and standing about 10 metres above the valley floor. These are ancient river gravels of the Ter, deposited when the stream profile was well above its present position. They provide convincing evidence of the reality of incision. The present channel, on the right as one descends, is now often dry due to the effect of the reservoir, and so offers an opportunity to study the work done by flowing water. Notice the highly irregular nature of the channel floor, the polished smoothness of joint-bounded blocks, the great variation in the size of the debris tools used by the river, and the way in which the present Ter has cut a narrow incision just below the surface of a wider, older channel floor. A glance to the north-east when leaving this section of the Ter reveals a distant view of a magnificent cuesta developed in gently tilted nummulitic limestone.

We have seen many examples of the work done by a river, but the more general theme of the interaction between rock type and sculpturing agents is important in Catalonia, and is particularly well demonstrated in the country around Olot, on the Upper Fluvia. Here, volcanic rocks have given rise to a striking landscape which has certain similarities with that of the Auvergne. Drive from Gerona towards the north-west, past Besalu, and then in a further 16 kilometres one will see to the left a cluster of houses perched above a precipitous cliff (Fig. 55). This is Castellfullit, the site of an intriguing episode of landscape history.

The steep cliff is developed on volcanic rock and at first sight it may seem that a lava flow simply occupied the present valley, and was then steepened by the erosional work of the river. However, there is evidence available to suggest a slightly more complicated history. It is possible, if awkward, to make one's way across the irrigation system and the river to inspect the junction between the lava and the underlying materials at the easternmost point of the flow. Surprisingly the lava rests on a layer of rounded gravels, now well above the present level of the river, but clearly laid down by an earlier Fluvia. Elevated fragments of the ancient rocky floor of that river can be seen nearby. The junction between gravel and lava is sharp and clear, shows no signs of disturbance, and the only obvious effect of the volcanic episode has been to bake some of the upper gravels. The evidence suggests that a lava flow occupied a valley whose floor stood several metres above the present level, and that the present river then cut down at the northern margin of the flow. The sheer face of the lava is a joint-controlled river cliff, cut by the Fluvia as it swung from side to side across its developing valley. Finally the river cut down to, and then below, the level of the ancient gravels.

The main road to Olot passes over the upper portion of the lava flow which, south-west of Castellfullit, is hardly dissected, and whose shape must therefore have changed little. This theme, of scenery being directly con-

Fig. 55. The valley of the Fluvia with the town of Castellfullit perched precariously on the eroded edge of a lava flow. At the base of the flow old river gravels can be found. Note the wooded valley sides and the development of terracing for agriculture on the lower slopes to the left.

trolled by volcanic activity, is well displayed in the vicinity of Olot. On the edge of the town is the fine volcanic cone of Montsacopa whose form has been altered more by quarrying than by the natural agents of erosion. However, an inspection of sections in the flanks of the cone suggests that the land surface generally slopes at a gentler angle than the dip of the ash and cinder beds, suggesting that the original slopes were rather steeper. The original crater is, however, perfectly preserved, and in autumn 1981 was being farmed for maize.

While the inland scenery of Catalonia is largely a result of rain and rivers acting on geological materials, an understanding of the coastal landscape involves an additional factor, the work of the sea. A glance at the map suggests that there are two types of coastline. The first is dominated by small sandy coves and rocky headlands, with pine-clad slopes rising steeply inland, and is well displayed east of Palafrugell and Bagur. The second consists of long, sweeping, sandy beaches such as Playa de Pals which are the seaward

Fig. 56. Columnar jointing in the basaltic lava flow of Castellfullit, northern Spain.

limits of low inland plains. Each type has much of interest to offer the observer.

The 'cove and headland' scenery can be investigated on various scales. On a large-scale view it is the result of the action of the sea on extensive outcrops of hard rock, but on a smaller scale the intricate coastal details reflect the importance of various planes of weakness in these resistant materials. One such resistant rock is granite, which forms much of the coastline between Tamariu and Lloret. The scenery of bays like Calella de Palafrugell and Llafranch provides fine examples of a coastal landscape developed in this particular rock type. Major lines of weakness in the granite have been exploited to form the bays themselves, while the adjacent headlands have withstood the attack of the sea more successfully. Throughout, the massive blocky nature of the granite can be seen, much softened in outline by the corrosive effect of rain and seawater. The beaches themselves are made up of granite products, which can be simply confirmed by picking up a handful of sand. Notice first how coarse it is; this reflects the size of crystals in the original rock. Then examine the individual grains: the vast majority are either translucent quartz, or pink or white feldspars. The micas have been weathered away. The beach is a result of the steady wearing away of the granite, and in addition provides the tools with which the waves can keep up a continuous attack on the coastline.

The small-scale joint systems of the granite are mirrored in miniature fashion by an even closer system of planes of weakness that affects the metamorphic rocks of the Pyrenean coast east of Puerto de la Selva, which have already been discussed from a geological point of view. Here you can investigate a most intricate coastline, whose narrow bays result from erosion along major planes of weakness. The country rock is, however, dominated by closely spaced foliations, only centimetres apart. These have been so corroded and roughened by rain and seawater that walking along the coastal fringe is quite difficult.

Occasionally, large-scale weaknesses dominate a section of the coastline. You can study a fine example just north of Estartit, beyond the harbour and its enclosing sea wall. Follow the coastal track as far as possible and then, to your left, you will see a magnificent cliff developed in limestone. Look closely at its face and you will make out many elongated patches of a reddish material, which appear to be recessed into the face of the cliff. You should also see near-vertical channels, often ending upwards in small overhangs, and lacking the reddish deposit, while at least one such recess contains a fine curtain of stalactites. This material, when combined with the geological findings, throws light on the history of this piece of coastline.

The evidence suggests that this cliff face has not simply been cut by wave action, but is close to an ancient, near vertical, plane of weakness in the limestone. This plane was corroded by percolating rainwater, which eroded channels and then locally formed stalactites. Later, during the Quaternary, the reddish topsoil was washed into these channels, together with frost-shattered fragments of limestone. The present cliff was finally revealed when earth movements thrust the mass of limestone to your left in a southerly direction.

A striking contrast in coastal scenery is provided by the long sand beaches of, for example, the Gulf of Rosas. Although this scenery may appear simple, the underlying causes are quite complicated and partly reflect geo-logical controls, which can be understood by consulting the map. The flat, sandy bays of the Gulf of Rosas and of the Playa de Pals are largely due to the presence there of soft, easily eroded Neogene sediments. Another factor is also at work, however. A glance at the topographic map will indicate that each bay is entered by an important stream, the Fluvia and Ter respectively. These streams have, over many thousands of years, brought down large amounts of sediment, subsequently distributed by the sea in the form of long, sandy beaches. South of Lloret, however, the position is rather different. The River Tordera has built a small delta, whose sandy and gravelly character makes for an ideal camping site, while further south the almost monotonously uniform coastline is developed on fine debris eroded from the granite hills to the interior.

Just inland from the coast there is good evidence for an episode in recent Earth history when a surface process, now relatively unimportant, was much more significant. Drive along the road from Pals towards Bagur, and after about 7 kilometres a thick drift of sand, now pine covered, comes into view on the left-hand side. Similar, more extensive deposits can be found mantling the south-facing slopes of the Santa Catalina hills between Estartit and Torroella. The best examples of all, however, are found in the Pyrenees, notably along the Cadaques road about 3 kilometres from Puerto de la Selva (Fig. 57).

Here thick deposits of weakly cemented sand can be seen, showing normal- and cross-bedding, and choking many small valleys. Occasionally, patches of a coarse, poorly sorted deposit, containing much angular material, occur within a sand sequence. It is worth looking closely at the sand grains with a hand lens to confirm that they are well rounded and well sorted.

This evidence indicates that the sand was deposited by wind, perhaps during a very cold period as the coarse, angular debris suggests that down-slope movement of material was occurring under conditions of freezing and thawing. The shape of the present landscape had already been formed, so a reasonable conclusion would be that the sands were deposited during one of the later glaciations of the Pyrenees, perhaps the last, when the low sea-level would reveal ample sand in the offshore zone.

A journey across east Catalonia, from the Pyrenees north of Ripoll, through the mountains around Olot to Gerona, and on to the Costa Brava in the vicinity of the Gulf of Rosas, will reveal surprising but characteristic

Fig. 57. Section through a fossil sand dune near Puerto de la Selva, eastern Pyrenees. The sand was probably deposited during the cold episodes of the later Quaternary. Note the cross-bedding.

132

differences in vegetation and rural land use. With regard to the vegetation, there are three basic zones, which reflect the climatic gradient from the cool, moist atmosphere of the Pyrenees and the flanking Catalan mountains, to the much hotter, drier coastal region. Above 1600 metres on the Pyrenees the vegetation is essentially sub-alpine and alpine in character, whereas on the lower slopes and on the high ground between Ripoll and Olot the plant communities have a distinct mid-European aspect. These green landscapes give way east of Olot to typical Mediterranean scenery, with vegetation that often seems scorched or wasted in the summer months. The precise nature of the vegetation within these zones can vary greatly, however, due to a long history of interference by man and his animals, superimposed on diverse combinations of aspect and soil type.

In the Pyrenees and the Catalan mountains various kinds of pasture and rough grazing are evident, but intensive agriculture is restricted to the better soils of the valley floors and basins. On the other hand, the coastal plains of Ampurdan, which focus on the market centres of Figueras and Gerona, presents a very different agricultural setting. Here cultivated land is pre-eminent and unmistakably Mediterranean in appearance, with vines, olives, and numerous irrigated market garden areas, or *huertas*. South of Ampurdan, as far as Barcelona, farming activity is confined to coastal areas and to the narrow depression or corridor between the coastal hill range and the Catalan mountains. Where river valleys break through the coastal hills, strips of cultivation link the interior depression to the coast.

The three vegetation zones referred to above occur within broad altitudinal limits, and these in turn correspond to ecologically significant contrasts of temperature and precipitation. In practice, of course, when making the descent from the Pyrenees to the coastal lowlands it will often be found that the altitudinal limits of a particular category of vegetation are modified, sometimes quite markedly, by the aspect and degree of exposure of the terrain in question. Furthermore, the changes from one plant community to another with decreasing elevation are seldom sharp; rather they are blurred by assemblages of plants which are transitional or mixed in terms of species composition.

On the highest parts of the eastern Pyrenees, above about 2300 metres, conditions are too harsh for tree growth. Bare rock and screes alternate with pastures, which, traditionally, have been grazed by sheep in the summer months. The flora is in fact alpine, and includes a range of small, low-growing plants that produce attractive flowers in spring and early summer. Below the high pastures mountain pine forms at first a scrub, and then, together with occasional silver firs, a rather sparse forest. On south-facing slopes especially, heaths in which dwarf juniper, broom, and bearberry flourish have replaced the forest, and there are also large tracts of grassland. Those which are dominated by the mat grass are pale-coloured and coincide with poor, acidic soils in the main. They contrast with the richer greens of the fine-leaved fescues, which tend to pick out the soils of better nutrient status. A reminder of the generally cooler and damper climate at these elevations are the boggy tracts, known as *molleres*, in which grow sedges and some alder. This sub-alpine belt of vegetation extends roughly down to 1600-metre contour, though analogous plant communities recur on certain of the pre-Pyrenean massifs, such as the Sierra del Cadi, and there are even limited examples much further to the south, on the summits of the Sierra de Montseny, south-east of Vich.

Between 1600 metres and about 1100 metres beech woodlands and a number of vegetation types derived from them are well represented, although nowhere are they very extensive. South of the Pyrenees proper they occur only in the mountains of Garrotxa, Ripoll, and Coll-sa-cabra, and reach their most southerly outpost on the higher slopes of the Guillerias and Sierra de Montseny. The beech is able to thrive in these areas because of the distinct maritime influences they experience, with frequent mist and low cloud. Indeed where such conditions prevail locally at lower elevations, as in the vicinity of Olot, for example, beech-clad slopes are found at just 600 metres above sea-level. Conversely, west of Ripoll, moist, maritime influences are less obvious and the beech is replaced by Scots pine. Much beech woodland has been cleared on the more gentle gradients for grazing land. The latter usually comprises heather-dominated communities on acidic, sandy soils and grassland on limestone substrates.

Below the beechwoods in the Pyrenees, and covering large expanses of the Catalan mountains southwards to some distance beyond Vich, are woodlands and woodland remnants in which the deciduous downy oak and sessile oak are common. Their eastward extension is, in comparison, very much more restricted. However, in both directions it is the long summer drought of the true Mediterranean climatic regime which more or less delimits the distribution of these two species of oak. Many of the shrubs and herbaceous plants associated with the deciduous oaks actually belong to the Mediterranean habitat, particularly where there has been considerable disruption of the woodland cover.

East of a line passing approximately through Le Perthus, Olot, and Vich, all but the highest ground was originally covered in woodlands of the evergreen holm oak. This tree has greenish-grey foliage and brown or blackish-brown bark. Young leaves and those on low shoots often resemble those of the holly, which is why, incidentally, the systematic name of the holm oak is *Quercus ilex*, from the Latin nouns for oak and holly respectively. In the least disturbed of the evergreen oakwoods the holm oak still grows to heights of 15 metres or more, and tends to cast a rather deep shade in which few shrubs can grow. Conversely, where the woodlands are more open, a rich undergrowth of shrubs is normally to be found, including varieties of cistus and such characteristic evergreens as the strawberry tree, box, juniper, laurustinus, Mediterranean buckthorn, the mastic tree or lentisc, and the tree heath. Climbing plants, particularly honeysuckle, clematis, and certain species of the genus *Smilax* usually grow in a tangled fashion over the shrubs. Beneath the trees and shrubs a range of herbaceous plants may be present, and many of these are evergreen as well. Since many of the shrubs mentioned show a distinct preference for either acidic or calcareous soils, they are likely to be encountered in different associations.

The destruction and exploitation of the evergreen oak forests of the Mediterranean Basin have continued over many centuries for this part of the world was the cradle of a number of ancient civilizations. Clearance and repeated burning to create and maintain rough grazings for sheep and goats have been widespread, and by eliminating or degrading the natural vegetation cover they have also led to severe soil erosion. Catalonia is no exception in this respect, although it does contain some of the least disturbed remnants of evergreen oak forest in the western Mediterranean.

As the woodland canopy was broken up and thinned out, the shrubs of the undergrowth were able to flourish as dense thickets ranging in height from 4 or 5 metres down to 1 or 2 metres. These shrub communities are referred to as *matorral* in Spain, *maquis* in France, and *macchia* in Italy. On limestones, the erosion of the naturally thin soils effectively prevented the development of the taller forms of secondary growth, and instead a low cover of shrubs generally much less than a metre in height and with much bare rock showing though was established. In France, vegetation of this type is known as *garrigue*, while in Spain there are several names in use, depending on the dominant plant. For instance, the *tomillares* are equivalent to *garrigue* in which thyme is especially abundant. The intensity of Man's impact on the landscape has varied greatly from place to place, so that in any one area the distinction between *garrigue*- and *maquis*-type vegetation may not always be clear.

In reality, then, the hillsides of east Catalonia which formerly supported evergreen oakwoods now carry an ever-changing mosaic of plant communities which differ in terms of age structure in addition to species composition and density. Away from the more remote and inaccessible places much of the remaining woodland is somewhat scrub-like in character, and apart from the holm oak the only other trees of any importance are the cork oak, the stone or umbrella pine, and, especially in proximity to the coast, the maritime pine. The exact ecological status of the pines in the original woodland cover is not known with certainty, but it seems likely that they were relegated to dry, infertile areas. In contrast the cork oak probably grew alongside the holm oak, yet it too has an obvious affinity for coarse-textured, sandy soils such as are formed on the granitic rocks of the region. The surviving holm oaks are generally small and gnarled, partly because of the man-induced impoverishment of the habitat and partly because the largest specimens are periodically cut for timber. The impoverishment of the habitat also allows the stone pine to compete successfully with the oaks. It has a dark, spreading, umbrella-like crown, while the trunk is typically short and divides into numerous branches. The cork oak is similar in appearance to the holm oak, but has less luxuriant foliage and a much thicker and more deeply fissured bark. Owing to the value of its bark, this tree has been widely cared for, and planted in a number of localities. There are quite dense woods of cork oak in the Sierra de Montseny, and the tree is also plentiful in the hills around Gerona, Palamos, and San Feliu de Guixols where it sustained a once-flourishing cork industry.

The scrub woodlands frequently merge into the taller type of *matorral*, in which there is often a dominance of one comparatively fire-resistant shrub, like the strawberry tree, box, mastic tree, or, quite commonly, bush-like forms of the holm oak. The latter are accounted for by the fact that holm oak regenerates freely from suckers after a fire. Where the human interference has been more profound or more recent the tall *matorral* passes into lower types, where shrubs such as cistus are much in evidence. They are readily combustible in the main, yet grow quickly from seed after burning, when the competition from larger shrubs has been suppressed. The derived plant communities of the limestone areas, and which approximate to the *garrigues* of France, are characterized by aromatic herbs and small, prickly shrubs. Typical representatives are rosemary, lavender, and thyme. While these limestone communities have a decidedly parched aspect at the height of summer, they can be very colourful when in flower earlier in the year.

The evergreen oakwoods and the numerous types of vegetation that have replaced them are well adapted to contend with the long summer drought. Many of the plants minimize their evapotranspirational loss of water into the atmosphere in one or more ways. The great majority of the dominant trees and shrubs have small, hard, leathery leaves, or sclerophylls – hence the term sclerophyllous to describe the Mediterranean vegetation in general. In the case of the pines the leaves are further reduced to needles. Evidently small leaves limit the surface-area available for evapotranspiration. Glossy leaf surfaces, which are another common feature, reflect a great deal of sunlight, so that the temperature immediately over the leaf, and thus the related evaporation stress, are lower than they might otherwise be. Additional adaptations include the ability to periodically close the stomata, or pores, through which the plant transpires, and the protection of the stomata with a covering of downy hair. Then there are the plants which give off an aromatic scent. They exude oils which again inhibit water loss, as does the excessive thickening of the bark in such plants as the cork oak. Apart form combating water loss, the perennial plants are, on the whole, also equipped to exploit the soil thoroughly for its reserves of moisture. In the main the root systems are extensive or dense, but in some instances there are deep tap roots. Finally, in this context, it should be noted that the two varieties of succulent plants which are sometimes so conspicuous on the most disturbed ground, namely the prickly pear cactus and the century plant (a species of agave), are native to the New World and are relatively late introductions to the Mediterranean region.

While large expanses of the Catalan hills retain some form of woodland or *matorral*, and convey a sense of wilderness, the lower slopes adjoining the major valleys, the plains of Ampurdan, and the interior depression, have long been cleared and in many instances terraced, for vines, olives and almonds (Fig. 58). The valleys and the lowlands themselves are nearly everywhere cultivated, usually with the aid of irrigation systems fed from wells and the rivers draining the hills inland. The farmland is a patchwork of fields devoted to a polyculture of maize, wheat, fodder crops, dairying, and some pig rearing. Trees of benefit to the farmers and their animals have been planted on the field boundaries, an example being the carob, whose clusters of large pods are fed to cattle. The irrigated *huertas* further diversify the rural landscape, and produce fruit, cereals, and vegetables for the nearby urban populations. Interestingly, there are even significant amounts of rice grown in that part of the Ampurdan basin adjacent to the Gulf of Rosas.

In general the tree crops are situated on the poorer soils unsuited to more intensive farming, and represent the more traditional elements in the rural landscape. On the other hand the growth of tourism and of the economy as a whole which Catalonia has experienced in the last two decades, has stimulated much innovation in the cultivated areas. Even so, the latter have

Fig. 58. Characteristic Catalan scenery near Hostalrich. The low ground is generally cultivated, with scrub on the shallower soils of the lower hillsides. On the hills proper there is a dense canopy of pine and oak.

retained their varied, irregular character, with innumerable small fields and plots growing a wide selection of crops and vegetables. This spatial diversity partly reflects the complex patterns of ownership which have emerged over the last 2000 years or more, and partly the fact that the farmers and smallholders include so many different crops in their rotations. In other words the everchanging small-scale fabric so typical of much of lowland Catalonia is an expression of the individualism of the people who live and work in it.

The landscapes of Catalonia fall into a number of categories which can be readily identified on a journey through the region. In the north is the high country of the eastern Pyrenees with its deep valleys and narrow, rocky ridges mantled by alpine plants. This scenery contrasts strongly with the almost featureless plains of Ampurdan further south which show an intricate pattern of farmland and irrigated plots supporting vegetables and fruit. Travelling across the plains one periodically crosses broad yet shallow valleys through which flow streams that are typically shrunken in summer. The Catalan hills, such as the Sierra de las Gabarras, make up a third landscape assemblage. They emerge abruptly from the plains and their vegetation cover shows an equally sharp contrast. Their slopes are locally mantled by stands of evergreen oak, but elsewhere scrub and matorral dominate, although the lower areas may be cleared and terraced for vines, olives, and almonds. The final landscape is the one most familiar to the visitor – the coastal fringe whose character is closely related to geological controls.

This apparently straightforward arrangement hides considerable complexity. Geologically, the region is part of the complicated collision zone between mainland Europe and the Iberian peninsula. The land-forms of the area show the importance of recent geological activity and bear the imprint of cold climate processes related to the glacial episodes of northern Europe, and the vegetation is not simply a response to a Mediterranean climate, but reflects some 2000 years of human interference.

7 Jutland

In contrast to the majority of areas described in this book Jutland is a lowland region, the surface of which has been extensively modified by glaciation. Glacial moraines, outwash, and windblown sands and peat bogs cover vast tracts of land and the hard-rock substrate is rarely exposed (Figs. 59 and 60). From Slesvig in the south to the middle of the Island of Mors in the north-east and Aarhus in the north-west, glacial and other recent sediments cover deposits of Miocene age. Along the east coast, beyond Horsens and Skanderborg, the Oligocene forms a narrow outcrop as far as Aarhus. There it swings inland and continues as a broader, but rather sinuous, outcrop as far as the eastern shorelines of the Limfjorden. Isolated outcrops of Danian rocks crop out south of Struer and Skive but the main outcrop of these early Cainozoic rocks occurs to the west of Hobro and east of Randers. Randers is sited on the Oligocene but on its northern outskirts a thin tract of Palaeocene represents the thin edge of a wedge-shaped outcrop that widens considerably on either side of Ebeltoft. Eocene rocks crop out on the Islands of Mors, Fur, and Live, and on the mainland around Logstor. The geological map of Jutland shows clearly that to move north is to move down succession; and that to the north of Nibe and Mariager are to be found the oldest rocks on the peninsula, the relatively recent Chalk of the Upper Cretaceous.

Most visits to Jutland begin from the town of Esbjerg, the major port on the western coast. It is an intriguing regional capital and an ideal starting-point for a tour of mainland Denmark. In terms of the geology of the region, this is confined to a limited number of quarry and coastal visits. However, all are extremely interesting and they provide a considerable amount of data on the environments that existed in ancient times. As much of southern and central Jutland is covered by Miocene sediments, it is a good idea to begin by visiting localities where these rocks can be studied. Miocene rocks crop out close to Esbjerg and a drive south to the town of Gram will take us to the type locality of the Upper Miocene Gram Clay. This is exposed in several old workings 1 kilometre north of Gram Castle. The quarries are accessible, in spite of some flooding, and numerous fossils can be collected. The Gram Clay is not a uniform deposit and, at the top of the section, you will notice that the clay is intercalated with fine silts. At the base the silt fraction is essentially missing. The green mineral glauconite normally laid down under marine conditions, is abundant. These sediments were laid down under marine conditions and the fauna consists mostly of molluscs and marine vertebrates. With time and great perseverance it is possible to collect 130

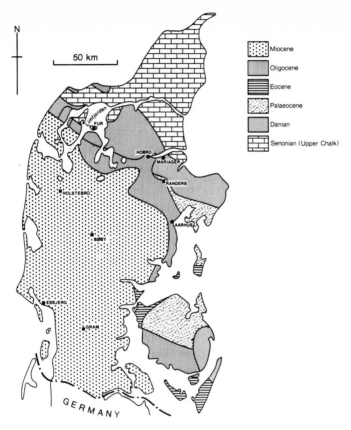

Fig. 59. A simplified map showing the solid geology of Jutland and the island of Funen.

species of bivalves and gastropods, with the genus *Astarte* being the most abundant form.

Crabs are also a common find at Gram, and the general indication is of a relatively shallow-water offshore community. The teeth of the sand shark *Odontaspis* and the vertebrae of the basking shark *Cetorhinus* are also common, and their presence tends to support the above hypothesis. The bones of turtles, seals, and whales (Fig. 61) may argue for an open, marine environment, however, particularly as the turtle *Psephophorus* is known to have been a cosmopolitan, or widespread genus. The seal bones belong to an animal similar to the extinct species *Pagophilus groenlandicus*, while those of the whales are referred to as the species *Mesocetus argillarius*.

Any visit to Gram should include a visit to the Midtsønderjyllands Museum. This is a new venture within the region and it more than adequately covers the geology of southern Jutland. Permission to visit the type locality can be obtained from the Museum curator and he will inform you

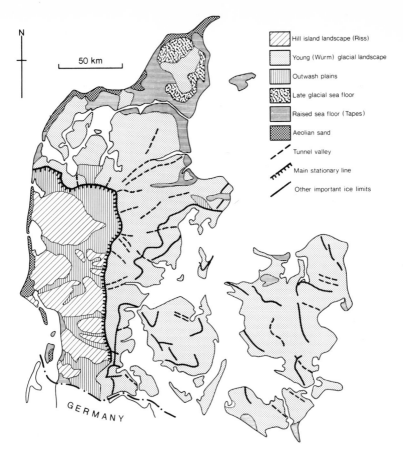

Fig. 60. The Quaternary landscape of Denmark. The main contrast is between the Riss 'hill island' landscape of west Jutland and the younger scenery elsewhere. These two zones are separated by the Main Stationary Line.

that, while the removal of molluscs, crabs, and sharks teeth is approved, the discovery of any large bones should be reported to the Museum.

In Denmark the Gram Clay sits on top of the Hodde and Odderup Formations. These represent the Middle Miocene and they can be studied in the old brown-coal working near Damgaard in central Jutland. Again these workings are subject to flooding and great care must be taken during any field visit. Where exposed the Odderup Formation consists of cross-bedded quartz sands, brown coals, and an upper sand unit. It is essentially a marine–deltaic sequence and reflects the change from an open marine environment to one of a landlocked, swampy basin. The brown coals are approximately 10 metres thick, with three distinct coal units interbedded with sands and silts. In the Upper Sand unit fine laminations are visible and a

141

Fig. 61. Vertebrate fossils are quite common in the Gram Clay deposits. This head and neck of a Baleen whale was discovered in 1979 and is dated at 5 million years old.

careful search may yield plant remains. In the past the Damgaard locality was renowned for its plant material and a comprehensive flora is known to contain species of walnut (*Juglans*), elm (*Ulmus*), willow (*Salix*), alder (*Alnus*), and pine (*Pinus*). Records also exist for the presence of asparagus (*Smilax*) and redwoods (*Sequoia*) and the suggestion is that the climate in the Middle Miocene was warmer than it is today.

In the upper part of the sequence the junction between the Odderup and Hodde Formations is marked by a basal quartz conglomerate. The Hodde Formation is characterized by black clays and inercalated sands and is capped by the *Astarte*-rich Gram Clay. Other outcrops of the Upper Miocene occur along the shores of the southern Limfjorden and once again certain species of the ever-present *Astarte* will help accurately to pinpoint one's stratigraphic position.

Around Nykjøbing it is possible to find outcrops of the Oligocene. These are also known from the Mariager Fjord and from localities just north of Aarhus. Both Middle and Upper Oligocene are characterized by glauconitic clays and from the upper Oligocene in the last two localities bivalves such as

Leda and *Meretrix*, and the gastropods *Pleurotoma*, *Fusus*, and *Apporhais* can be easily collected.

The search for fossils may be continued on the beautiful and peaceful island of Fur. Here, too, there is an excellent local museum and a visit will help in understanding the geological phenomena exposed on the shoreline. Fur is essentially composed of Eocene rocks draped with glacial sediments. The rocks however, are different from those of the Paris and London Basins and a detailed investigation will reveal that they consist mainly of diatomaceous clays and volcanic ash bands (Fig. 62). The two have a varve-like appearance and whereas there are 39 ash bands in the lower part of the sequence, 140 are present in the upper 27 metres. This contrast may reflect changes in the frequency of volcanic emissions. The rocks of Fur are part of the Mo Clay Formation and they are the time equivalents of the London Clay.

The Eocene of Fur is therefore interesting from both an environmental and palaeontological point of view. But most impressive are the fold structures that occur as a result of glacial tectonics (Fig. 63). At first sight the area looks as though it has been affected by the Alpine Orogeny. A closer investigation of the Mo Clay and the overlying glacial materials will soon correct this view. (This theme is developed in the section on landforms.)

On Jutland and the eastern islands of Denmark excursions can be made to see the unique 'Bryozoan limestone' of the Danian. This deposit sits on top of the Upper Chalk (Maastrichtian) and is best seen in the classic localities of Faske and Stevns Klint. As Faske the limestone is exposed in a large quarry and, with permission, it is possible to study several sections of the fossiliferous Middle Danian. In hand-specimen it can be observed that the sediment is disctinctly chalky in texture and that often it consists mostly of bryozoan debris. These are small colonial organisms with a delicate lace-like appearance and in many areas of the quarry occur in distinct banks. The limestone is rich also with the skeletons of brachiopods, serpulid worms, and scleractinian corals. At the base of the main workings the corals occur as large colonies with the aptly named *Dendrophyllum candelabrum* as one of the most common species. Strangely the surrounding sediment rarely infills the spaces between the coral branches although none of the colonies are in the upright 'life' position. On many corals brachiopods are found cemented to the branches. This is thought to have taken place when the branch itself had died. Other brachiopods occur as distinct 'nests' with the sediments and there are the remains of numerous bivalves and crustaceans. In the more compact limestones of the Flaske quarry the remains of corals are still common. Large cavities linked with the burrowing activities of crustaceans are also common to these horizons, and other traces in the form of sponge borings are also present.

The bryozoan limestones are therefore exceedingly rich in terms of fossils,

Fig. 62. Alternating light and dark bands are characteristic of the Mo Clay Formation. The dark bands represent periods of volcanic activity; with volcanic dust from events sited in the Skaggerak being carried in a predominantly southwards direction. (*Photo by Eric Schon Jensen.*)

and the evidence they provide indicates that the sediment was laid down in water no deeper than 80 metres. In has also been estimated that the water temperature at the time in question was around 28 °C. Over the years these Danian limestones have been referred to both the Cretaceous and the Cainozoic. Lithologically they resemble the underlying Chalk but much of the palaeontological evidence suggests that they should be regarded as Cainozoic. At the present time the majority view seems to favour the latter.

Of all the landscapes described in this book, that of Jutland is among the most recent. It is dominated by Quaternary events, and more particularly by the impact of the last major north-European glaciation (the Weichsel) which began about 70 000 years ago and finally ended a mere 12 000 years BC. As

Fig. 63. Ice-induced fold structures within the Mo Clay Formation, Hanklit, Mors, Denmark. (*Photo by Eric Schon Jensen.*)

the ice age melted a further series of landscape-forming processes began their work, and have continued through to the present day. You might think that Jutland's youthful scenery implies that it was fashioned in a rather straightforward manner, but close investigation reveals a story as complex as that for any European region we have described.

The major impact of glaciation was to lay down an extensive cover of drift deposits on which the present scenery is developed. This drift veneer is of variable thickness: it averages about 50 metres for the country as a whole and reaches a maximum of 291 metres at Frederikshavn in north Jutland (Fig. 64). It follows from this that rocks older than Quaternary have made a negligible contribution to the landscape. As we have already seen their influence has been indirect, and they have rarely had any effect on the actual shape of the land surface. For example, the peninsula of Djursland in east Jutland owes its existence to the relative height of resistant Danian limestone, while the details of its relief are glacial in origin. The same argument applies in west Jutland, where the high ground around Bulbjerg and Svinkløv is developed on Danian limestone and Senonian chalk respectively, while the surface form reflects glacial activity.

A more detailed look at the scenery will allow identification of three major land-form assemblages, of rather unequal importance. The country

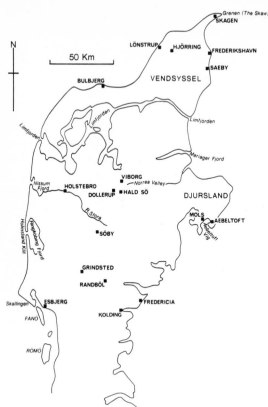

Fig. 64. Location map of Jutland.

east and north of Esbjerg, whose lowlying uniformity is suddenly broken by abrupt 'hill islands', constitutes a first scenic unit, while the rest of Jutland, dominated by low, irregular hills and wide valleys, provides a second recognizable unit. Danish scientists have identified a clear boundary, the Main Stationary Line (see Fig. 60), between these two units, and this term suggests a reason for the contrast in scenery. The coastal region, dominated by dunes, fjords, and extensive flat surfaces makes up the third and most recent of the landscape assemblages, and is a result of late glacial and post-glacial events.

Inland from Esbjerg the scenery is relatively simple. The dominant impression is of an extensive plain, whose gradient is barely perceptible, and which laps against abruptly emerging hills. This landscape assemblage is well displayed east of Holstebro, where the fine hill island of Yllebjerg stands above the plain which has been incised by the flat-floored valley of the Stora. The wide plain of Randböl about 20 kilometres east of Grindsted in Central Jutland offers a further good example, in this case locally mantled by inland sand-dunes.

The key to understanding the origin of the hill island landscape has been provided by detailed investigations of the land surface. Careful survey has shown that a typical 'plain' is made up of one or more nearly flat fans, whose outer gradients are about 1:1000, and whose apices, steepening to 1:700, generally coincide with the Main Stationary Line. Ice of the last glaciation advanced as far as the Line and then, as the climate became warmer, great volumes of meltwater were released and flowed away to the west, depositing huge, low-angled outwash fans. The Icelandic term 'sandur' is often used to describe such broad sand and gravel spreads. The hilly landscape that developed as a result of the preceding Saale glaciation was partially buried. The unsubmerged hill islands were modified by processes that operated during and after the cold Weichselian episode, and also by meltwater as the ice thawed so that their original shape has been completely changed. This hill island landscape is the oldest in Denmark.

North and east of the Main Stationary Line the character of the landscape changes. The extensive outwash plains of south-west Jutland are now much reduced in importance, and are associated with steep-sided hills, hollows lacking outlets, and impressive valleys, many of which appear far too large for the streams that now occupy them. Most landscapes are the result of erosional forces acting on the underlying rocks, but that of north and east Jutland is the almost unchanged consequence of the haphazard dumping by a melting ice-sheet of the load it was carrying. A close inspection of the landscape components, beginning with the nature of the glacial deposits themselves, will provide much evidence about the detailed way in which it was developed.

Almost any roadside cutting will provide information about glacial and post-glacial processes. A section through hilly moraine, especially if it is near an ice margin, normally reveals coarse drift that has had its finer particles removed by meltwater as the ice decayed. Such a deposit is usually stratified. Elsewhere an exposure of clayey moraine will usually reveal an upper horizon, about 4 metres thick, showing a yellowish-brown colour which contrasts with the dark grey to greyish-blue hue beneath. The lighter colour is due to oxidation of ferrous to ferric compounds, and is a measure of the importance of weathering in the post-glacial period. The moraine itself contains cobbles and boulders, many of which have a local origin, but far-travelled erratics which originated outside Denmark are occasionally to be found. If the origin of such an erratic can be determined it is called an indicator boulder, and the study of a large number of these has enabled scientists to build up a picture of the various directions of ice advance. The discovery of rhombporphyry from the Oslo region, of porphyry from Dalecarlia, and of Østersø quartz porphyry from the floor of the Baltic near the Åland islands has helped to build up a picture of changing directions of ice advance during the last glaciation.

Certain coastal sections provide striking evidence that throws light on the behaviour of an active ice-sheet. The sea cliff of Lönstrup Klint near Hjörring in north-west Jutland shows a fine development of about 100 tilted glacial beds, each consisting of meltwater sands, silts, and clays, and referred to as floes. Each bed dips towards the north–north-east, which is the direction from which the ice advanced. This imbricate arrangement resulted when active ice broke up a formerly continuous layer of glacial sediments and rearranged the floes so that they dipped up-glacier. A similar pattern, though of course on a much smaller scale, occurs in river deposits. A very similar arrangement can be seen in cliff sections exposed through marginal moraine ridges around the west part of the Limfjord in north-west Jutland. Here the floes are of Eocene Mo clay and of Oligocene mica clay. In this situation the direction of ice pressure was towards the south.

The character of the land-forms themselves is a direct response to the nature of the icesheet mechanisms, in that each distinct element of the landscape was fashioned by a particular glacial process. Perhaps the most distinctive unit is the undulating ridge country which is associated with periods when the Weichsel ice margin remained relatively stable during its long retreat. Sections through the hills show that the drift has typically had the finer particles removed, and when it is bedded there are many signs of later disturbance. This type of evidence suggests that the irregular ridges are terminal moraines, locally washed by meltwater as the ice began to melt back, or dislocated by a bulldozer effect as the ice temporarily advanced. In addition to the Main Stationary Line scientists have identified two further terminal moraines in east Jutland, and more further east.

You can examine a fine terminal moraine some 3–4 kilometres in width in the vicinity of the inlet of Aebeltoft Vig, south Djursland. The road from Aebeltoft northwards passes through the hilly landscape of the Handrup terminal moraine. The hills in this region stand some 20–30 metres above the adjacent depressions and about 90 metres above sea-level. Natural sections have often been exploited for gravel. Around Mols on the west side of Aebeltoft Vig the moraines are of the thrust type, reflecting a local ice advance during the last glaciation. As a consequence they possess a strikingly steep-sided character, enhanced by powerful meltwater erosion. Figure 60 suggests other localities where similar terminal moraine landscapes may be examined.

The landscape developed to the east of the main terminal moraines frequently presents a much smoother appearance. A particularly large example may be inspected in the area of Fredericia in south-east Jutland. Here the scenery shows gentle, irregular undulations, and was fashioned by the smoothing effect of ice advancing over a clayey moraine. This ice-smoothed 'moraine flat' was relatively unchanged during deglaciation as very little debris was deposited during the melting episode. A variety of the moraine flat is occasionally found at a higher altitude, when it is called a moraine plateau. In this situation it is typically dissected by post-glacial stream activity, and you may again inspect examples in the vicinity of Fredericia.

Tunnel valleys are to be found in much of Jutland, and Figure 60 shows the location of the major examples. A fine illustration is offered by the Kolding Å valley near Kolding in East Jutland. This valley is particularly helpful in connection with the problem of the development of the 'tunnel' landscape. The present stream flows eastwards, making large, meandering swings across the flat valley floor. Scientists have demonstrated, however, that the direction of flow of the stream that cut the original valley was to the west, that is, against the gradient. A very similar arrangement occurs at Hald Sø, south of Viborg. Here the long profile of the tunnel valley is remarkably uneven and as a result the present valley is occupied by lake-filled hollows and elongated bogs in the depressed stretches, and by morainic undulations in the elevated sections.

There has been much debate among scientists over the origin of the tunnel valleys. One influential body of opinion holds that the valleys were cut by meltwater flowing beneath the ice towards the glacial margin at the Main Stationary Line. The escaping meltwater may well have flowed through braided channel systems. This is suggested by the occasional islands that occur within the tunnel valleys, such as the island of Øby in the Nørrea valley. It is pointed out that the Weichselian ice-sheet was probably several hundred metres thick, and so a considerable head of water could be established within the ice as melting got under way. This 'hydrostatic pressure' may have been sufficient to force subglacial meltwater streams uphill for considerable distances. As the streams left the ice margin they deposited the debris load they were carrying to form the extensive outwash plains of west Jutland. For example, the large fan at Dollerup was laid down by streams draining four large tunnel valleys that converged near Viborg.

Other investigators have disagreed with this interpretation. They have pointed out that in the case of Hald Sø valley the gradient is such that a subglacial stream would have had to climb through a vertical distance of some 113 metres. They argue that this is not very likely, especially as the ice margin was close and so the sheet would be quite thin and unable to support high, subglacial water pressures. The alternative view is that the tunnel valleys were cut by direct glacial erosion, which would be focused along the lines of already existing shallow valleys. It is clear that the debate over the origin of the tunnel valleys of Denmark is not yet closed.

Whatever their origin, these valleys have in many cases been modified by processes acting in the late- and post-glacial periods. For example, the tunnel valley of the Norrea near Øby about 14 kilometres east of Viborg, was both modified by meltwater after the Weichselian ice-sheet melted and then invaded by the sea during a marine transgression. Its floor has been levelled still further by the depositon of fjord sediments.

The pattern of scenery that we have investigated in Jutland tends to be repeated, in varying proportions, throughout the Danish islands, and a journey towards Copenhagen from Jutland reveals a recurring series of familiar features. There is, however, one remarkable feature of deglaciation that is only properly developed east of Jutland. You will occasionally find long, sinuous hills, whose height is remarkably uniform for considerable distances, extending along tunnel valleys or over the surface of moraine plains. These features are called eskers. Morgenstrup Aasen and Strö Bjerge on Sjaelland, and Grindlöse Aas on northern Fyn are the largest and best known eskers in Denmark. Their origin has stimulated much discussion. Legend has it that they were deposited by a 'goblin with a leaking sand bag', but modern scientists take a more sober view of their development. A commonly held view is that eskers are the beds of subglacial streams which, during the final stages of ice melt, were unable to carry the material with which they were supplied. This interpretation links tunnel valleys and eskers as the two extremes of subglacial stream behaviour.

The third main landscape assemblage of Jutland is that affected by post-glacial marine and coastal activity. You will find the development of the associated scenery quite easy to understand if you keep in mind the significance of two associated themes: changes in the relative height of land and sea during the post-glacial epoch, and the contribution of various agents of erosion and deposition.

The area of north Jutland offers the best examples of landscapes fashioned as a result of changes in sea-level. Figure 60 reveals that extensive tracts are occupied by raised sea floor. The road between Frederikshaven and Saeby runs over such an elevated floor, and the associated ancient cliffed coastline can be clearly seen away to the west. A further good example, though rather less accessible, occurs midway between the inlets of Mariager Fjord and Limfjorden in the area of Lille Vildmose. This theme of land emergence in north Jutland contrasts with the situation in the south-east, where the drowned ends of tunnel valleys provide a typically fjord coastline. A brief outline of late- and post-glacial history is essential for the understanding of this contrast in coastal landscapes.

Towards the close of the Weichselian episode the area of northern Jutland was depressed by the weight of overlying ice. The Earth's crust responds rather slowly in response to changes in pressure and so the land remained depressed when the ice finally melted away. This allowed much of north Jutland to be invaded by a late glacial sea between about 13 000 and 10 000 BC. The deposits of this sea form a sandwich, made up of a lower sand, associated with the beginning transgression, the Yoldia Clay (named after the cold-water mollusc *Yoldia arctica*) which was laid down when the water reached its maximum depth, and an upper sand laid down as the sea was shallowing. The land surface now began its delayed rise in response to the removal of the ice, and the associated retreat of the sea lasted until about 6500 BC. The climate was by now much warmer than at the close of the Ice Age, and sea-level rose as melting ice in the northern hemisphere released water to the oceans. This second transgression (by the Tapes Sea, named after the mollusc *Tapes decussatus*) reached its peak about 3000 BC in north Jutland. The final event, which is still continuing, is one of marine retreat as the Earth's crust continues its recovery. This recovery is not, however, uniform. Since the Tapes peak it has been greatest (about 13 metres) in the extreme north of Jutland, where the ice was thickest, while a line of zero recovery runs between Nissum Fjord on the west coast and Fredericia in the south-east.

This sequence of events has important implications for the coastal landscape. Much of Vendsyssel in north Jutland was invaded by the late-glacial sea, resulting in the development of marine plateaux standing some 30–35 metres above present day sea-level, and surmounted by morainic hill country. The valleys dissecting the plateaux are therefore much younger than those incising the hilly regions and have much steeper and fresher sides. At Kvissel, west of Frederikshavn, the plateau has been so dissected that its flat character has disappeared, while west of Saeby are plateau fragments several square kilometres in area. The later Tapes transgression resulted in an extensive development of raised beaches finely displayed in the vicinity of Frederikshaven. South of the line of zero emergence since 3000 BC the coastline has been dominated by the post-glacial rise in sea-level. The drowned tunnel valleys of south-east Jutland are a result of this rise.

It should not be forgotten that recent and contemporary marine processes are busily fashioning the coast of Jutland. Material eroded from one locality may be deposited at more suitable sites to produce spits, such as the Skaw, and bars like Holmsland in front of Ringkjøbing Fjord in west Jutland. Short-term investigations have however revealed a slightly different pattern. Comparison of eighteenth- and twentieth-century maps has shown that erosion is tending to dominate over accretion. It appears, for example, that the Skagen peninsula is now being eroded, even though it is slowly rising as the Earth's crust recovers from the weight of ice.

The second major feature of the coastal environment is a dune landscape. This is particularly well developed in west Jutland, where it occupies a belt up to 10 kilometres wide extending between the northern promontory of Grenen (The Skaw) and Skallingen, opposite Esbjerg. The dunes continue on the islands of Fanö, Mandö, and Römö. The location and development of the dune system are the result of the combination of a number of favourable features. There is an ample supply of sand, originating as glacial debris. This dries out readily in suitable weather, and then blows freely. The pattern and intensity of winds provide a ready explanation for the westerly location of the dune systems. The most frequently occurring winds are from the west, and gales are almost always from this direction. The result is that sand is steadily blown inland to form the contemporary dune complexes. Constant wind pressure implies that some areas will ultimately have their sand cover completely blown away. The resulting feature is called a deflation plain, and an example may be seen at Rabjerg Stene, Vendsyssel, north Jutland. This plain is developed across the raised sea floor of the Tapes transgression. It has been stripped of its sand cover and of the finer marine deposits, and is now veneered by a layer of pebbles that inhibit further erosion.

Much of the scenery of Jutland has been fashioned within the past 15 000 years or so, but this short history hides a remarkably complex sequence of events. The key to understanding the development of the landscape is to be found by a study of the behaviour of the declining Weichselian ice-sheet, but subsequent events have also made important contributions.

The array of Quaternary deposits and land-forms which typify so much of Denmark have exerted a marked influence on the history and character of its rural land-use patterns. This relationship is evident not only on the local scale, but also at the regional level, where there is a distinction between the landscapes of the older moraines in the western half of Jutland, south of Limfjord, and those of the younger moraines, which occupy much of the rest of Jutland and all the larger islands except for Loesø and Bornholm. Yet despite the importance of physical controls, the contemporary rural scene, which is dominated for the greater part by highly productive farmland, is several stages removed from the original woodland cover in which oak and beech flourished. Indeed, such woodlands as exist today are often planted, and with conifers rather than hardwoods.

The only other landscape elements of real importance, apart from those developed on the moraines, are associated with the coast – which is hardly surprising, perhaps, in view of the great length of Denmark's coastline in relation to its limited land area. There are large tracts of former sea floor in the north and east of Denmark which in many cases now support fertile farmland. In contrast are the extensive accumulations of sand-dune and salt marsh, particularly along the Atlantic seaboard, for they present a rather desolate aspect, although less so in those districts where the marshes have been reclaimed for agriculture.

Fossil pollen evidence and the distribution of certain types of archaeological remains reveal that the earliest phase of forest clearance for farmland occurred in west Jutland during prehistoric times. The conversion process began in the Neolithic period, continued into the succeeding Bronze Age, and in the Iron Age was already far advanced. This part of Denmark proved attractive to prehistoric farmers because the light, sandy soils which are widespread on the plains of glacial outwash, were best suited to their primitive agricultural implements. The generally much clayier soils of north and east Denmark were not cleared until heavier ploughs were in use, well into the first millennium AD.

As we have seen elsewhere in Europe, cultivation of sandy soils can soon deplete their nutrient reserves and, in the absence of adequate manuring and fertilization, they become increasingly acidic. Degradation of this kind led to the early widespread abandonment of farmland on the sandy soils of west Jutland, and the emergence of featureless expanses of heathland in which the chief plant was heather. Such heathland, with occasional copses or scrub of oak and birch, relieved in places by the older morainic hill islands characterized much of west Jutland until the latter part of the nineteenth century. The bulk of it was given over to rough grazing, principally for sheep. Farming communities and settlements were largely confined to the better soils of the river valleys and certain of the larger hill islands. Where marginal tracts of the adjacent heath were brought into cultivation, they were farmed on a rotation which included a fallow period ranging from five to twenty years in length, so as to allow the sandy soils to recover their modest fertility. Peat bogs were common in the depressions on the heaths and traditionally were cut for fuel. Over the last hundred years so much heathland has been transformed into smallholdings and farms that sizeable examples of it can now be found only in conservation areas.

Although the territory of the younger moraine was put under the plough much later, it has remained in continuous agricultural production right up to the present. Even so, far-reaching changes in the farming pattern have also taken place here, but the changes were initiated at an earlier date. In the early eighteenth century the feudal system of farming still held sway. Most of the land was in large estates owned by landlords and, to a lesser extent, by the Crown. Most of the farmers were tenants and worked strips scattered over three large, open fields located around the village. From about 1760 onwards there were attempts at a more rational organization of the land, and in order to eliminate some of the obstacles which had been experienced, far-sighted laws on land reform were passed in 1781 and 1793. All the lands relating to a village, including the outlying commons, were pooled and subdivided into new parcels on the basis of productive capacity, so that a parcel on formerly uncultivated or common land was larger than those on the better soils. Farms and farm buildings were then moved out of the village on to the more distant of the reorganized units of land. By 1815 virtually all the farm land on the younger moraines had been dealt with in this radical fashion. Thus, over much of Denmark we have a pattern of ancient villages, with many much more recent detached or outlying farmsteads.

In general a somewhat uniform agricultural mosaic came into being, interrupted only where particular combinations of relief and soil type discouraged farming activity. This is most apparent in the morainic hill country, especially if steep slopes coincide with stony or sandy soils. In these situations woodland and heath frequently alternate with pockets of cultivation in the depressions or, where drainage is bad, with lakes and bogs. In the same way, woodland and scrub often cover the sides of the deeper tunnel valleys and meltwater valleys. Conversely, the morainic flats, such as the 'Heden' south-west of Copenhagen and the 'Sletten' north-west of Odense, tend to correspond with featureless plains of intensive agriculture. On the islands some diversification is provided by the eskers which rise above the flats. Since these winding ridges of sand and gravel also support many stands of timber, they are usually very conspicuous features in the landscape.

The reclamation of the heathlands of west Jutland was, in part, stimulated by the major land reforms of the late 1800s and early 1900s, but a far greater impetus to agricultural improvement was the loss of Schleswig-Holstein and its good farmland to Prussia in 1864. The Danish Heath Society was founded two years later, and under the motto 'what was outwardly lost shall be inwardly won', embarked upon the colonization of the great heathlands of Jutland. With government assistance, it undertook deep ploughing to break up the subsoil hardpan, huge quantities of marl were applied, peat was removed and burned, and drainage was regulated. In all, about 700 000 hectares were reclaimed for farming, and 25 000 new holdings came into being, along with new 'station towns' or market centres. Denmark's agricultural area was increased by roughly a third, while the planting of nearly 200 000 hectares of trees – mainly coniferous and in orderly plantations – also doubled her forested area. Rather than heath, therefore, the typical scenic elements now are fields, often divided by north–south oriented screens of conifers to protect from wind erosion of the soil, and gale damage to crops in this windswept land, together with scattered blocks of dark conifers. The new, straight roads constructed as part of the reclamation programme are further reminders of the relative youth of the farmland of west Jutland.

Land reform and heathland reclamation helped lay the foundations of Denmark's highly productive agricultural economy. At first, corn was widely grown and exported, and some of the windmills dating from this phase in the country's development are still dotted around the landscape, particularly on the morainic hills and ridges. Cheap grain from the vast wheatlands of north America, however, compelled Danish farmers to turn to animal husbandry for their livelihood in the last quarter of the nineteenth century. The need to compete and export foodstuffs at competitive prices encouraged the establishment of numerous cooperatives, for dairy products, bacon, eggs, cattle buying and selling, and seed supplies. Such organizations enabled individual farmers to obtain the economic benefits of large-scale enterprise.

By 1950 there were about 200 000 farms and smallholdings in Denmark, practically all of them having a variety of livestock reared on the produce from an eight-course rotation of grass, grains, and root crops. Since 1950 this patchwork of arable and pasture has changed considerably. In response to economic pressures and technological innovation average farm sizes have increased. This has been achieved through farm amalgamation, although the decline in the number of farms, to below 120 000, is also a result of the loss of land to urbanization. The size increase has been accompanied by a marked tendency to specialize in cattle, pigs, and, to a lesser extent, poultry. Market gardening, too, has become more important around the major towns and cities. Corn now occupies about 60 per cent of the ploughed land, and roughly 80 per cent of the area under corn is actually devoted to barley, largely for livestock feed. In effect, then, the overall trend as in other European countries has been towards greater monotony in the rural landscape.

Turning finally to the coastal environments of Denmark, the flat expanses of raised sea floor in the north of Jutland and in the north of Zealand are cultivated in the main, while woodland and scrub often pick out the old cliffs which, in places, define the limits of the flats inland. Similarly, where the soils are very sandy or gravelly, sparse and frequently heathy vegetation is more likely than farmland. In fact there are also remnants of once-extensive peat bogs which formed as a result of the poor natural drainage on these planate land-forms. Most of the bogland has been drained and improved for agriculture, yet its original area can generally be reconstructed from the fact that villages and individual homesteads were restricted to the adjacent dry ground. This influence on the settlement pattern can readily be detected in the Lille Vildmose district of Himmerland.

The contemporary maritime environments include the sand-dunes and salt-marshes which are so characteristic of the western coast of Jutland. Here the dunes form almost continuous ramparts up to 10 kilometres wide. Under the influence of the prevailing westerly wind the dunes have encroached upon farmland and villages, and in this century there has been appreciable planting of conifers and marram grass in an effort to check any further advance.

The salt-marshes and associated tidal flats are best developed along the south-west coast of Jutland, in the region known as the 'Vadehavet'. Here the glacial outwash plains of west Jutland present to the sea an extremely low-lying expanse of fine-grained sediments. The tidal range in the Vadehavet is between 1 and 2 metres, yet since the slope of the outwash plain is so gradual, large areas are flooded at high tide only to be left dry again as the tide falls. Tidal flats of this sort provide ideal conditions for the colonization of salt-marsh plants. Southern Jutland is sinking slowly so that some coastal drowning has also taken place. The former position of the coastline south of the Skallingen is picked out by the islands of Fanö, Mandö, and Römö, in the lee of which there are further tracts of salt-marsh.

The salt-marsh meadows of the Vadehavet have traditionally been grazed by sheep, cattle, and horses, though this is less in evidence now as farming generally has become much more intensive. However, reclamation of the marshes for agriculture has gone on since medieval times, by the erection of dykes to exclude the sea. The approaches to Esbjerg, are actually flanked by extensive sand-dunes and salt-marshes.

The landscapes of Jutland are unique among those described in this book, in that the solid geology has made virtually no contribution towards their development. Quaternary events, and especially the impact of Man, have been the dominant formative influences.

The greatest contrasts in scenery are between the hill island terrain of west Jutland and the newer morainic landscape of the east, which are separated by the Main Stationary Line. In simple terms these two regions are underlain by contrasting Quaternary deposits. In the west great outwash fans have given rise to sandy soils, readily depleted of nutrients, whereas in the east, Man has had to contend with much heavier clayey material directly deposited by decaying ice-sheets. West of the Main Stationary Line, a large-scale nineteenth-century colonizing effort saw the reclamation of former extensive heathlands and their replacement by a landscape pattern of cultivated fields, conifer screens and stands, and straight roads. The heavier country to the east has been continuously cultivated since its clearance and tends to show a uniform agricultural mosaic partly resulting from land reform at the close of the eighteenth century. Diversity is provided by patches of woodland on the steeper slopes of the tunnel valleys and by lakes and bogs that occupy closed depressions.

The influence of Man is everwhere apparent but has not been able entirely to eliminate variations that are due to the impact of later Quaternary events.

Glossary

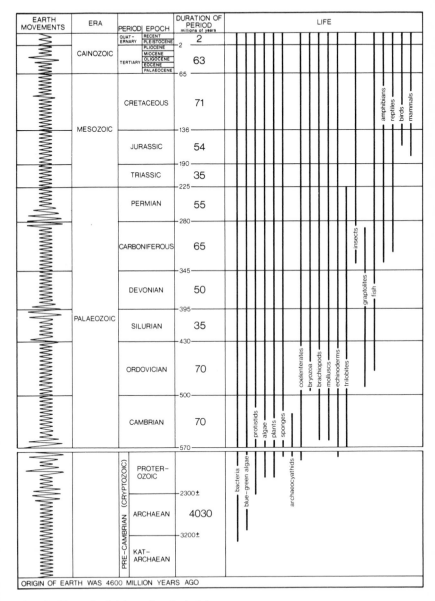

Fig. 65. The main divisions of geological time.

Glossary

Alder-carr woodland: fen or swampy woodland dominated by alder.

Allochthonous: a term used to describe rocks formed from materials which have been transported or displaced tectonically.

Alluvium: a variable deposit laid down by a river.

Antecedent: describes a stream whose course was established before a phase of Earth movement and then successfully maintained in spite of the disturbance.

Anticline: an up- or arch-fold in stratified rocks.

Arete: a steep sharp-crested ridge. An important variety is formed by the meeting of two adjacent cirques (*see* cirque).

Autochthonous: a term used to describe rocks formed from materials which have not been transported, and which have not been displaced by thrusting are referred to as autochthonous.

Basement: a foundation of igneous and/or metamorphic and/or strongly folded rock beneath a cover of sedimentary rock.

Basic: means relatively poor in silica. Basic rocks tend to weather readily and to produce more fertile soils than those with plentiful silica.

Batholith: a large intrusive body of rock, usually granitic, with a surface expression in excess of 100 square metres.

Bedding plane: a plane or surface within a rock which represents an original depositional surface.

Belemnites: an extinct group of molluscs which are related to squids, cuttle fish, and octopi. Their hard parts are frequent in certain Mesozoic deposits. The most common fossil remains of these animals are the shiny, bullet-like guards.

Blanket bog: a carpet of bog mosses (**sphagnum**) with other plants growing on and through it. Beneath the carpet, peat occurs. Blanket bogs occupy extensive areas on planate summits in upland Britain, though they have been much altered by burning and grazing. There is little doubt that the growth of blanket bogs was initiated by prehistoric farming activities.

Braided: the condition of a river when discharge is carried by several channels that separate and rejoin rather than by one single channel.

Breccia: a rock with gravel-size angular fragments set in a finer-grained matrix.

Butte: an isolated hill left behind by the irregular retreat of an escarpment.

Calcicole: a plant with a marked affinity to lime-rich soil.

Carbonates: rocks rich in carbonate minerals such as calcite, aragonite, and dolomite. May be deposited as direct precipitates of sea-water or formed by the 'fixation' of minerals by plants and animals. Some carbonates are accumulations of skeletal remains.

Cheire: confused microrelief which represents the congealed surface of a lava flow.

Chlorite: a greenish mineral resembling mica in some respects and is found in igneous, sedimentary and more especially in metamorphic rocks.

Cirque: an armchair-shaped hollow produced by glacial erosion. Local names for the same feature are: corrie (Scotland), cwm (Wales), botn (Norway).

Clastic rock: are sediments made up of the debris of pre-existing rocks.

Clitter: a deposit of angular granite fragments ranging up to the size of boulders, strewn over the valley sides of Dartmoor.

Community: a group of organisms occupying a particular area. A community is usually named after one or two of its most obvious or numerous species, or after the habitat.

Conglomerate: essentially rounded gravel-size particles cemented into a coherent mass.

Coombe rock: a Pleistocene surface deposit made up of chalk rubble with some flints in a matrix of fine chalky material. It is derived from the Chalk and is the product of frost action and solifluction (or sludge-creep).

Coppice-with-standards: the name given to woodlands which for centuries were managed for their oak standards and hazel coppice.

Couloir: a steep shallow valley in a mountain region often swept by avalanches.

Crinoids: examples of the so-called 'spiny-skinned' animals, the Echinodermata. They are characterized by a skeleton made up of calcareous plates and have a complex water vascular system. Most skeletons consist of a cup with arms and a long stem.

Crystophylline: the term generally applied to a basement complex consisting of igneous and metamorphic rocks.

Cuesta: an asymmetric ridge possessing one gentle and one steep (scarp) slope. Normally caused by a resistant stratum dipping at about the same angle as the gentler slope.

Diatomaceous: a term applied to sediments rich in the remain of diatoms, which are planktonic algae found in fresh- and salt-water.

Dip valley: a valley tending down-dip; often characteristic of the dip slopes of cuestas (*see* cuesta).

Drumlin: a streamlined land-form made of glacial sediments and formed beneath an actively advancing ice-sheet.

Dyke: a sheet of igneous rock which has been intruded more or less vertically into the rocks through which it passes. Such an intrusion cuts across stratification where it is present.

Ecosystem: the interrelation of living things with each other and with their physical environment.

Epidermis folding: refers to folding that has taken place in the outer, younger layers of the lithosphere above the basement.

Fluvioglacial: laid down by meltwater associated with a decaying glacier or ice-sheet.

Geosyncline: an elongated trough in the ocean floor adjacent to the margin of a continent in which great thicknesses of sediment accumulate. As the weight of sediment increases so the floor of the geosyncline subsides.

Gneiss: an irregularly banded, crystalline metamorphic rock. Coarse bands of whitish minerals alternate with thin, typically discontinuous layers of dark minerals.

Graben: a block which has been let down between two parallel faults but which unlike a rift valley, need not have any topographic expression.

Greywacke: coarse-grained rock comprising particles of sand-size in a matrix of finer particles.

'Hagging': the dissection of peat bogs by dendritic drainage networks to produce very difficult terrain. 'Hags' or islands of uneroded peat separate the drainage channels, which eventually cut down to the base of the peat. Whether this dissection is natural or man-induced is not clear.

Hassock: a soft sand found between the layers of calcareous sandstone in the Lower Greensand of Kent.

Head: a Pleistocene surface deposit, formed by solifluction under periglacial conditions and typically found on valley sides and valley bottoms. It is heterogenous in composition and grain-size, and may display layering.

Glossary

Horst: a block between two parallel faults which has been uplifted relative to the adjacent rocks.

Ice Age: name given to the last 1.7 million years of earth history dominated by periodic glacial advances (glacials) and warmer intervening episodes (interglacials). The last glacial is known as the Devensian (Britain), Weichsel (N. Europe), or Würm (Alps).

Imbricate: the term means overlapping. It is applied to thrusted sheets of rock all dipping in the same direction and having similar displacements. The obvious analogy is with roof tiles. Another use of the term is to describe the relationship between fragments of rock or pebbles deposited by water currents.

Inlier: an outcrop of older rocks surrounded by younger rocks.

Inverted relief: a land-form whose present shape is the opposite from that it possessed originally, as a result of subsequent erosion. An example is an original anticlinal hill, now breached by erosion to form a valley.

Kentish rag: a hard calcareous sandstone which occurs in beds in the Lower Greensand of Kent, the beds being separated by soft sand or hassock.

Klippe: the remnant of a nappe or pile of nappes, separated from the parental body of rock by erosion or gravity gliding.

Lahar: a flow of mud derived from volcanic deposits. The water in the flow may derive from rainfall or from a crater lake.

Limestones: rocks rich in calcium carbonate, most limestones forming at the present are in the form of the unstable carbonate aragonite. After deposition this changes to calcite and most ancient limestones are composed of the latter (*see* carbonates).

Limon: the French name for former wind-blown material which has been degraded by weathering.

Loess: a silt-rich, light coloured wind-blown deposit. In Europe during the Pleistocene, extensive sheets of loess were deposited south of the glaciers. Rock flour produced by glacial abrasion was an important ingredient of the loess.

Magma: molten rock which may occur within the Earth's crust, or upon it – when it is referred to as lava.

Malmstone: a siliceous rock containing many sponge spicules which is often found in the Upper Greensand.

Metamorphic: the term applied to rocks which have been altered by heat and/or pressure.

Metamorphic aureole: the belt of metamorphosed rocks encircling a formerly deep-seated igneous intrusion.

Mica: a silicate mineral with perfect cleavage into very thin layers or 'leaves', which have a mirror-like lustre. Some micas are black or dark shades of red or brown, whilst others are colourless. They are formed by igneous and metamorphic processes, but derived mica grains are also found in sedimentary rocks.

Migmatization: a process associated with intense metamorphism, in which some of the rocks melt to form mobile granitic material which interacts with the unmelted rock. The result is a rock with mixed characteristics, partly granitic and partly metamorphic.

Misfit: a stream occupying a valley that is disproportionately large and must therefore have been eroded under different circumstances.

Molasse: freshwater or continental rocks deposited after a phase of mountain building.

Mont: a hill formed by an anticline.

Moraine: an accumulation of glacial deposits. May also refer to land-forms of glacial deposition, e.g. the terminal moraine formed at the terminus of a glacier.

Mylonitization: a process of grinding and shearing commonly associated with the thrust planes of faults, which produces a banded or streaky rock with a very close texture known as mylonite.

Nappe: a structure in which the rocks have been folded and thrusted horizontally for distances measured in tens of kilometres.

Nummulite: a single celled animal which secreted a chambered, disc-shaped outer test. Nummulitid tests are particularly common in certain Eocene limestones and clays.

Olivine: a silicate mineral which generally lacks cleavage but which possesses conchoidal fracture. Olivines range in colour from green, brown–green to yellow–green.

Oncolith: a finely laminated rounded structure formed by algae that live or lived in the tidal zone. Calcareous muds are gathered to the outer surface of the algal ball as it rolls around over the substrate.

Ooid (or **Oolith**): a spherical concretion arranged into concentric layers around a nucleus. Limestones composed of carbonate ooids or ooliths are known as oolites.

Ophiolite: probably part of the basaltic ocean floor which has been thrust on to continental margins.

Orthoceras: an extinct relative of the living *Nautilus*. A straight-shelled cephalopod.

Orogeny: a period of mountain building

Outlier: a detached mass of rock, separated from the main outcrop of that rock by rocks which are geologically lower (usually older).

Overstep: refers to sedimentary sequence deposited by a transgressive sea. Each new bed of sediment extends farther onto the old land surface than its predecessor.

Palaeogeographic province: a faunal province is a region characterized by a particular assemblage of animal life; a palaeogeographic province is one which existed in the geological past.

Pediplain: a variety of planation surface cut by the erosional action of non-channelled surface water flow under a semi-arid climate.

Phyllite: a metamorphic rock resembling slate on the one hand and schist on the other. It is coarser grained than slate, and like schist, is rich in mica.

Pillow lavas: lavas extruded on to the sea floor cool rapidly on the exterior of the flow into pillow-like structures.

Planation surface: a topographic surface with little available relief which has been worn down by the processes of erosion.

Planèze: a planate, elevated land-form which corresponds to the sloping surface of a lava flow.

Pyroxene: a rock-forming silicate mineral. The pyroxenes are a large and varied group.

Refuge: an area above the tree-line, with soils that have relatively large reserves of nutrient, where plants of the tundra which covered much of Britain in late-glacial times have been able to survive through the ensuing post-glacial.

Sandstones: sediments formed mainly as a result of the fracture and breakage of rock debris. Their grain-size is 0.06 to 2.00 millimetres and the majority are quartz-rich. Sandstones are clastic rocks (*see* clastic) the grains of which are moderate to well rounded and commonly cemented by either quartz or calcite cements.

161

Glossary

Schist: a coarse-grained metamorphic rock rich in mica. The mica minerals have a sub-parallel orientation and so impart an irregular fine-scale foliation.

Screes: a more or less cone-like deposit of mainly angular rock fragments derived from the weathering of exposed rock surfaces above. Individual screes often merge to give an apron-like accumulation.

Serpulid worms: calcareous tubes deposited by the polychaete worm *Serpula* are known from sediments ranging in age from Silurian to the present.

Sill: a more or less horizontal sheet of igneous rock which has been intruded along rather than across the stratification of the rocks in which it is enclosed.

Slaty cleavage: is a property of some fine-grained rocks and describes the fact that they cleave or split readily into thin plates. The platyness is derived from compression and is aligned at right angles to the direction of compression.

Spilitic lavas: submarine lavas that have a pillow structure due to rapid cooling and considerable chemical alteration because of interaction with the sea-water.

Stratovolcano: a volcano made up of an alternatively layered sequence of relatively viscous lavas and pyroclastic debris.

Strike vale: a valley eroded along the strike of a soft sedimentary layer.

Structural degradation: high acidity tends to destroy the clay particles which help bind the soil together. Humus similarly acts as a kind of glue, sticking soil particles together into stable aggregates. Prehistoric farming methods in the uplands of Britain and on sandy terrain in the lowlands frequently led to acidification and the loss of humus.

Syncline: a down or U-fold in stratified rocks.

Terrace: a nearly flat surface especially of an old flood plain left behind by river erosion.

Trilobite: an extinct marine arthropod with head, thorax, and tail regions.

Turbidites: a sediment laid down in water by turbidity currents. Such a sediment is coarsest near its base and fines upwards. This is because the lowest and densest parts of the current flow faster than the upper parts of the current and so transport the coarsest grains.

Val: a valley formed by a syncline.

Varve: a seasonal increment of sediment on the floor of a glacial lake. Spring and summer water bring in a fresh supply or sediment, the coarser material rapidly falls to the bottom, whilst the finer material settles out over the remainder of the year. Thus one varve or one year's layer of sediment comprises a relatively coarse-grained basal part grading upwards into finer-grained material. Other sediments with well defined layers are also referred to as being 'varved'.

Villafranchian: a European subdivision of geological time, spanning the late Pliocene and early Pleistocene.

Wave-cut platform: a gently sloping offshore platform formed by the abrasive action of waves and often exposed at low tide. Typical of cliffed coastlines.

Würm: name given to the last Alpine glaciation which lasted between about 70 000 and 10 000 years ago. Occasionally used to refer to the last glaciation in other regions.

Location Index

(Including geographical features)

Aa (Valley) 18
Aarhus 139, 140, 142
Abbey Wood 5
Aber 58
Aebeltoft (Ebeltoft) 139, 146, 148
Afon Ogwen 58
Aiguille Rouge de Varens 35
Aiguilles Rouges 38
Aisne 21, 23
Alessandria 35, 46
Allagnat 115
Alps 12, 31, 33, 35
Alun, Côte d' 25
Alum, Côte d' 25
Amange 26
Ampoix 108
Ampurdan 118, 120, 121, 125–7, 133, 137,
    138
Ampurias 122, 126
Andover 63
Angles 126, 127
Aosta 35, 41–3
Aosta, Val d' 42–4
Apennines (Ligurian) 46–7
Arcets 31
Arenthon 34
Argentière 40
Argentière, Glacier d' 38
Arras 17, 18
Arve 34, 36–41
Arvier 41
Ashdown Forest 7
Avants Monts 28
Aveyron 38
Aydat 100
Aydat, Cheire d' 111
Aydat, Lac d' 111
Ayse 34

Bagur 118, 124, 129, 132
Bangor 52
Banyuls-des-Aspres 119
Barcelona 124, 133
Bar le Duc 24
Barnstaple 78
Bars, Côte des 25
Bars Cuesta 25
Bars, Plateau Des 24, 25, 27

Barthod, Combe 32
Bas-Boulonnais 15, 17
Beaulieu 65, 66
Beaune 113
Beaunit 101
Beaunit, Maar De 108
Beddgelert 48
Bellever Tor 84, 85
Belvedere de la Chatelaine 29
Bembridge 66, 68
Berru, Mont de 18, 21, 22
Berry Head 77
Besalu 126, 128
Besançon 28
Besse en Chandesse 108
Bethesda 48–50
Béthune 17, 18
Betteshanger 11
Biella 44
Bienne 31
Bigbury Bay 84, 89
Billaude 30
Bilques 18
Blackgang 70
Blackingstone Rock 84–6
Bodmin 78
Bodmin Moor 78, 80, 82–4, 88, 92
Bognor 63
Bois d'Aldit 107
Bolt Head 77, 84
Bolt Tail 84, 89
Bonanay 38
Bonneville 34–6
Bormido 46
Borne (River) 36
Borne-Aravais, Massif de 34
Bornholm 152
Boscastle 81
Bossons, Glacier des 39, 41
Boulogne 11, 14, 24
Boulonnais 11, 12, 13, 14, 15, 17
Bournemouth 63, 64, 66–9
Bovey Tracey 78, 83
Bowerman's Nose 84, 85
Bracklesham (Bay) 64
Brading Down 67
Bray, Pays de 11
Bréche (Nappe) 36

163

Location Index

Location Index

Subject Index

The definitions of many of the terms listed below will be found in the Glossary

allochthonous 29, 37, 122
alluvium 45
Alpine earth movements 11
antecedent 31
anticline 11, 14–15, 19, 31, 38
arête 39
ash, volcanic 104
atrio 104, 106
aureole, metamorphic 82
autochthonous 29, 37

basement 41, 96, 98, 99, 100, 101, 102, 123
batholith 82
bedding plane 50
bomb, volcanic 100
braided river 36, 126–127
butte 20–21, 105

carbonates 14
cataclasite 119
cheire 107, 114
chert 2
cirque 38
cleavage 79
clitter 85–86
Coombe Rock 6, 12
coppice 73
coppice-with-standards 93
cross-stratification 27
culm 81
cuesta 6, 7, 9, 21, 25, 26, 27
cumulo-dome 104
cwm 53–54

deflation plain 152
delta 64, 80
dip 27, 46
downland 17
drift 67
drumlin 33
dry valley 19, 29
dune 95
 U-shaped 94

égeulé 104
enclosure 73, 74
epidermis folding 31

erratic 147
escarpment 20, 21, 22, 24, 25, 27, 32; *see also* scarp
esker 150, 154

fan 36, 43
fescue 59, 134
floodplain 3, 28–29
flysch 36

garrigue 135, 136
geosyncline 79
graben 28, 30, 97, 103, 109
grassland 91
 acidic 61

hagging 91
hardpan 154
heathland 66, 71, 72, 75, 92, 153
horst 109
humus 9

inlier 14, 15, 16

klippe 34

lahar 101, 102, 109
landes 112–14
liesegang ring 124
limon 19

macchia 135
maquis 135
mat grass 61
mattoral 135, 136, 138
meander 23
mesa 20
metamorphism 28, 79, 82
misfit river 23
moder 9
molasse 34
molleres 134
montagnes 114, 116
moor grass 61
moorland 90, 91
moraine 34, 36, 38, 39, 40, 41, 43, 44, 56, 57, 58, 139, 152, 153
 terminal 148